Bob Cowin

REFUGEE
COUNTDOWN

A Canadian – American Partnership to Resettle a Syrian Family

CLOSELY BASED ON A TRUE STORY

BOB COWIN

 FriesenPress

Suite 300 - 990 Fort St
Victoria, BC, V8V 3K2
Canada

www.friesenpress.com

Copyright © 2019 by Bob Cowin
First Edition — 2019

ISBN
978-1-5255-6568-7 (Hardcover)
978-1-5255-6569-4 (Paperback)
978-1-5255-6570-0 (eBook)

1. RELIGION, CHRISTIAN LIFE, SOCIAL ISSUES

Distributed to the trade by The Ingram Book Company

For David and Steven

TABLE OF CONTENTS

Preface   vii

Deciding to Sponsor   1
    Seattle Beginnings   1
    Potluck Lunch   5
    Decision Time   11
    Official Launch   21

Key Players   25
    Visitors from the South   25
    Metamorphosis   32
    Broadening Horizons   36
    Becoming a Team   45

Learning about Refugees   55
    The Refugees' Plight   55
    October Chatter   58
    More and More Learning   70
    Networks   78

More Active Engagement   83
    The Sister Who Wasn't   83
    Seattle Bound   94
    Refugee 101   100
    Next Steps   115
    Connecting with Lebanon   120
    All That Jazz   129
    Catching Up   131

Waiting Calmly with Occasional Jitters   **143**
    Health Scare   143
    Road to Emmaus   146
    Political Advocacy   150
    Still Waiting   152
    Yoga   154
    Movement   159
    Nesting Instinct   161
    Furnishings and Snail Mail Money   169
    Bring on the Bishops   171
    Saturday Evening Conversation   174
    Preach It, Sister   181

Final Preparations   **185**
    Arriving Soon   185
    Home Sweet Home   188
    Travel Arrangements and Graft   192
    Odds and Ends   196
    Countdown   205

Epilogue   **211**

PREFACE

Vancouver, Canada

The letter arrived in 2011 and could not have been more unexpected. A local Muslim family was asking our Lutheran church to sponsor their Iraqi relatives as refugees to Canada. The Canadian family would cover the considerable costs if we would just agree to sign the sponsorship papers. The United Nations and Canadian government, not us, would determine the eligibility of these refugees to enter Canada.

How and why this occurred is a story in itself, but not our current story. All you need to know for now is that we eventually agreed, and an Iraqi refugee family, the Badawis, arrived in November 2012 after months of waiting. To our considerable relief, we increasingly came to think we had made the right decision in helping out. We were not the perfect sponsors, nor did our refugee family adapt effortlessly to their new country. There were periods of befuddlement, resentment, and heartache, but also times of blessing and personal growth.

As the years passed, these Iraqi newcomers came to do as much to help us understand what Jesus meant when he spoke about the Kingdom of God as we had done for them in that first year when they landed in Canada. They, of course, would probably not use this language and may not even be aware of how subtly powerful their mere presence and gracious manner have been over the long term.

In any event, we came to see ourselves less as their patrons and more as their partners—a reciprocal relationship emerged that we had not anticipated. Though our paths were separate in many ways, the points of convergence enriched us.

The other background to our current story also dates from 2011 when the bloodshed in Syria began in earnest. A new Canadian government, elected in 2015, promised to bring a large number of Syrian refugees to Canada by what felt like "the day after tomorrow". We were interested and sympathetic to the humanitarian intent but wondered about the wisdom and practicality of the campaign promise. As we were a small congregation with limited financial capacity, we watched and did nothing.

We were once again caught off guard when another refugee sponsorship request came our way early in 2016. By the end of 2015, with the American government far from achieving its goal of resettling even a modest number of Syrian refugees, some committed individuals in Seattle had been thwarted in their efforts to help displaced Syrians. They eventually decided that, though they were blocked from directly helping Syrian refugees enter the United States, they could perhaps find indirect ways of providing assistance. If they could arrange for us to receive the $25,000 the Canadian government required for the first year of a private refugee sponsorship, would we help a Syrian family come to Canada instead of the United States?

This is the story of that second request: how it originated and what we did in response to it. Although the refugee crisis precipitated this story, the focus is not on Syrians but on us as sponsors, on the sponsorship process, and on the development of a relationship between congregations in two countries. We entered this endeavour not as complete novices, but the reality was that, as a group, we were not very sophisticated sponsors. We offer our learning from this experience in the hope that it will be of interest and benefit to others. We recorded our experiences to remind ourselves of the unexpected ways in which God's grace became evident to us.

Although names have been changed, some details altered, and literary devices employed, such as the invention of dialogue, the following account strongly reflects actual events.

DECIDING TO SPONSOR

Seattle Beginnings

On September 3, 2015, the newspaper image of two-and-a-half-year-old Alan Kurdi's body, prostrate, his face partially submerged in water on a beach in Turkey, galvanized the world to the plight of Syrians. "The most heartbreaking photo of 2015," *Time* magazine said. His death, and that of his mother and five-year-old brother, instantly became the poignant symbol of a refugee crisis. Because his Aunt Tima lived in the outskirts of Vancouver and had been trying to bring her relatives to safety, Syrian refugee policy skyrocketed as a political issue in the Canadian federal election campaign.

A year after Alan's death, Tima reported that the boy's father, her brother, was living in Northern Iraq, his mental health deteriorating. She had managed to get enough funding, refugee sponsors, and governmental permission to bring only one other brother and his family to live with her. But even this development had turned bittersweet as the siblings mutually decided they could maintain a better relationship by living apart.

In August 2016, Tima told the *Vancouver Sun* newspaper that the outpouring of compassion inspired by her nephew's death had been short-lived. She said Canada and the world had the capacity to do so much more. A few people had even accused her brother of being a human smuggler who was responsible for the deaths of his own family.

Not everyone's compassion was short-lived, however. Like many people, Seattle teacher William Mulgrew had been touched by the photo. "We have to do something," he declared. Unlike many, he actually did do something.

William and his husband, Karl Golds, started investigating what support they could provide Syrian refugees. They contacted local relief agencies and, although no organization directly said that they couldn't resettle Syrians, it didn't take William and Karl long to realize they were receiving a polite bureaucratic brush-off. Nationally, the American government set a humanitarian target of accepting 10,000 refugees from Syria—a modest goal, some argued, given the wealth and population of the United States. Others claimed it wasn't wise to bring into the country traumatized individuals who might be unsympathetic to American values. In any event, progress towards meeting the 10,000 target was exceedingly slow.

Feeling stymied, Karl flicked on the television and caught a newsclip of the new Canadian prime minister, Justin Trudeau, at an airport welcoming Syrian refugees to Canada. *Were things different in Canada than in the United States,* he mused, *and might Canadian involvement be a way of providing aid?*

During the previous autumn's election campaign, Trudeau promised to bring 25,000 Syrian refugees into Canada by the end of 2016. The promise both delighted and panicked the immigration agencies that would be doing the screening and providing logistical support to successful applicants. It was a massive commitment, but Trudeau's party had won the election and was now doing all that it could to fulfill its promise. "Sunny ways, my friends," Trudeau said in his victory speech, claiming that Canadians had clearly signalled their distaste for the politics of fear and divisive, mean-spirited policies.

Over the years, Karl and William had been involved to varying extents with Mount Olivet Lutheran Church in Seattle, an activist church with a long history of commitment to social justice issues. The international organization it was associated with, Lutheran World Relief, founded in 1945, had a good reputation and considerable experience with helping refugees. Karl left a message with the national Canadian branch in Winnipeg, wondering if a door was opening.

Karl received no reply, at least not promptly. He contacted the western office in Vancouver, which advised him that a Canadian church not too far from Seattle had previously sponsored Middle Eastern refugees and was looking to do something for Syrians. Perhaps, with the relief agency's help, he should contact the pastor, Ellen Thompson.

Karl didn't know that the information he received was only partially correct. Although the agency may have hoped the suburban Vancouver church, All Saints, was seeking to sponsor more refugees, it was a stretch to suggest vague thoughts in the minds of a few individuals was the intention of the entire congregation. Making what was essentially a cold call, he contacted Pastor Ellen and was able to convince her it was worth having a preliminary discussion. As coincidence would have it, or perhaps not so coincidentally some might say, Ellen was about to travel to Seattle to attend a conference.

At their meeting, Ellen was intrigued by the prospect of a partnership between two churches to help refugees. But, sighing, she cautioned that All Saints had no financial capacity to take on this project, as lovely an idea as it might be.

"What if we did all the fundraising here in the States?" Karl asked. "I'm sure we could get the money and figure out how to send it to you in a way that is above board. I'm a lawyer, after all, so I could find a way to make the transfer. Could your church look after the face-to-face contact with the refugees, with as much support from Seattle as we're able to provide?"

"Hmmm," Ellen replied. "Let me chat with some key people and find out what I can. I've never heard of such a cross-border arrangement, but there's nothing wrong with blazing new paths. I think the Canadian government requires something like $2,000 a month to support the family for the first year as they learn a new language and culture under a private refugee sponsorship agreement. Could you really send us that kind of money, even if the exchange rate continues to work strongly in your favour? One Canadian dollar only costs you about eighty American cents right now."

"Definitely," Karl said, wondering where exactly the boundary lay between confidence and fantasy.

One does not blithely send large amounts of money across international borders, especially not if tax deductible charitable receipts are to be issued to donors. If this idea of a cross-border partnership was to have any hope of being realized, it would have to begin with a legitimate vehicle in the United States for collecting funds. The obvious candidate was Mount Olivet church, given that routing the money north of the 49th parallel was likely to have some degree of Canadian Lutheran involvement.

Next came the chicken-and-egg task of laying the groundwork for fundraising.

"Would you be willing to donate a substantial amount if we could get an international partnership in place?"

"Are our Canadian partners committed? Who are the Syrians we would be helping?"

"The partners won't commit until they know the money is in place. And until they're committed, nobody will know who the Canadian government will allow us to help. Will you give us enough assurance that the Canadian church knows we're real?"

After several weeks of testing the water, Karl contacted Pastor Ellen. "Yes, I'm confident we can get whatever money is needed to sponsor a family," Karl reported. "What more can we do to help All Saints decide if it's willing to take this on?"

Potluck Lunch

All Saints is an unremarkable church in suburban Vancouver with a fluid attendance of sixty-five on a typical Sunday morning. Despite its roots as an ethnic establishment church in Northern Europe, the congregation attracts individuals from a variety of faith backgrounds, including those who are searching and uncertain about their beliefs. Preferring to look forward rather than back, it belongs to the more liberal of two main Lutheran denominations in Canada.

The involvement of All Saints with Syrian refugees began with a vague hope that the money it lacked to support refugees during their first year in Canada would not be a problem.

"I think there are a lot of people in the wider community who have the money and desperately want to help these suffering people but don't have an organizational vehicle to do it," one member said. "We could be the vehicle. It's not all that different from what we did a few years ago when the Iraqi family approached us with money to privately sponsor their relatives."

Early in 2016, rumours began circulating that Pastor Ellen knew activist lawyers in the United States who would fund Canadians to bring in Syrian refugees. Big on social justice, these lawyers were concerned that American borders were not open to Syrians.

"Well, not quite," Pastor Ellen said. "There is indeed a lawyer who I've talked with, but he's part of a church in Seattle. I'm surprised, but God may be opening doors for a cross-border partnership. My sense is that we at All Saints would be okay with sponsoring more Muslims, but I know some believe we should try to help Christians instead."

Informal conversations within small groups continued, and Ellen stayed in touch with Seattle. Finally, the musings became strong enough that a potluck lunch was arranged after Sunday worship on March 6 for a general discussion about refugee sponsorship—but not about a particular proposal. The previously sponsored Iraqi refugees, the Badawi family, were invited to the meal.

The warm hum of relaxed conversation grew among the diners seated in the multipurpose room. Off in the kitchen, however, the discussion in a small huddle sounded more frantic.

"Our guests of honour, the Badawis, haven't arrived yet, but people have started eating already. What's wrong with us?"

"Is there any food left that we can put aside for them?"

"It's not about the food. It's basic courtesy."

"And where are they going to sit when they arrive? We don't even have a place for them."

"It's under control. You can relax. We've put some plates of food in the oven to keep warm, and they're all *halal*. I'll get somebody to set up two tables over there in a vee-shape so it doesn't seem exclusionary. This isn't great, but we'll get by."

The discussion portion of the event had yet to begin when the Badawi family appeared. Partha held the door so that his wife, Zrebar, could enter with a large tray of sweet pastries. Their teenage son, Khaled, followed with another dish, and then Yasamin. They shyly smiled a greeting as three or four people rose to receive them.

"Welcome, welcome. We're so glad you're joining us."

"Here, let us take your tray. You can hang your coats right here and then I'll take you to your table. We have another group using this space at two o'clock, so we've started eating to ensure there's plenty of time for a meeting before we have to leave. We've just begun, though, and we'll bring some food to your table. Your dishes are halal and okay for Muslims to eat."

"Thank you," Zrebar said, taking the lead. Her English was stronger from the brief time she spent in the United Kingdom as a child. "We're hoping our friends, the Qatabs, will join us. Because they live nearby, they said they could find their own way here. I think that's brave because I don't know if they've ever been in a church before."

Ten minutes later, while people were still eating, Shayla Dunbar stood to start the meeting.

"Feel free to get more food and drink while I talk. Our time is limited, so let's begin our discussion." She explained that one of the purposes of the gathering was to talk about the church's previous experience sponsoring refugees. "The Badawi family has come to tell us more of their story; namely, what it's been like for them these past few years, after our formal sponsorship ended. This is vital information as we try to decide whether we as a congregation are willing and able to embark on another sponsorship." She then recapped the events of the past several years for those who had recently joined the congregation or not been involved with the previous sponsorship.

Shayla turned to Zrebar. "Could you tell us what you're currently doing? I think we would all benefit from your current experiences."

"Well," Zrebar said, looking first at Shayla and then her husband, "I help refugee families from all over the world through Welcome House in Vancouver. The biggest challenge is finding apartments to rent that are affordable and large enough. Because of the exchange rate, any money the families bring with them does not go very far. Refugees sponsored by the Canadian government, in contrast to private sponsorships, have the hardest time finding housing. Many of them still live in hotels, even weeks after arriving in Canada.

"I also help at the local food bank. I advise the other volunteers about acceptable foods for Syrian cultural and religious practices, and I show Syrian families how to use and prepare Canadian food. White flour, olive oil, sugar, black tea, thyme, which we call *zata*, and whole milk for the children are the most important staples. They are in short supply or completely unavailable at the food bank. It's hard to come to a new land and not have the comfort of familiar food."

While Zrebar talked, Judi quietly circulated with honeyed pastries the Badawis had prepared. "Maybe dates in the centre," she whispered to those who looked suspiciously at the unfamiliar nibbles. Others were happy to experiment.

"And now, could you tell us a bit about your own family's experience in coming to Canada?" Shayla asked. "Could you help us understand how Canadians can provide better support to newcomers?"

Zrebar thought for a moment. "When we came to Canada," she said, "all we could bring with us were the clothes we wore and a bag with clothing and belongings. We carried other things, though. All children and adult refugees have lived through the emotional trauma of war and we carry it with us for a long time. However, good experiences in Canada can help change these memories for the better.

"In our culture, we are surrounded by family. We don't really need friends because our extended families are so large. So we learned that, when we came to Canada, William and Annie Neufeld, Pastor Ellen and your congregation would become our family. We view you as much more than friends, and we are forever grateful for what you have done for us. You were constantly willing to help us.

"We Iraqis have lived through many wars. We are survivors. For the Syrians, however, this is their first war, and they are very afraid and distrustful. Food is crucial to their survival, and learning English is the next biggest task because most Syrians do not have any background in English."

Partha spoke next, briefly describing his experience in Canada and emphasizing that finding work is important but can be very difficult. Because of work-related injuries, he was looking for a new type of employment. "While I am doing this, I also volunteer with the local social services agency, SHARE, and help with resettlement through the Immigrant Services Society."

"Thank you so much for all that you've told us," Shayla said to Partha and Zrebar. "I think most of you know that Annie and William provided much of the help to the Badawis when they first arrived. William is here, and I wonder if you could give us your reflections."

William nodded. He walked to the front of the room, paused to collect his thoughts, and then spoke slowly. "I think the Badawis' settlement went quite well, despite the many challenges thrown their way. Some policies of the Harper government made life difficult for refugees. Government departments, for example, often took months to reimburse doctors for the services they provided to refugees. Doctors therefore became reluctant to take refugees as patients.

"Other rather mean-spirited policies included the requirement that refugees repay the cost of flights and medical examinations within three years. That was around $8,000 per family, making it very difficult for newcomers to become financially stable. My understanding is that some of these policies are changing under the new government.

"The All Saints welcoming committee had to wait a long time for the Badawis' arrival, then scramble when they came on very short notice. During the months of waiting, the lives of some committee members changed. Annie and I felt it was easier or necessary to do most of the organizing ourselves. Sometimes we had to act quickly, and consulting with a committee would not have been productive.

"You know, once you get involved, it doesn't have an end date. People come to trust and rely on you, even as they become more independent. Having Zrebar's sister, Munira, and her family close by made their beginning easier. However, when that family moved to a good job in Dubai, the Badawis were left with Munira's furniture but no family support.

"Partha was polite when he talked about the difficulty of finding jobs. Canada does not make things easy for refugees to work in their own field of expertise."

"Thanks, William," Shayla said as he wove back through the tables to his seat. "Time is passing, so I think we need to wrap up soon. I'll remind you that Pastor Ellen thinks we need to decide within the next ten days or so whether we want to proceed with

9

a Syrian sponsorship under the conditions outlined in the emails we've all received. This includes the Seattle lawyer and his friends raising $25,000 to be held in trust by Canadian Lutheran World Relief. We'd help with getting kids enrolled in school, opening a bank account, showing them how to shop, and so on. And just plain offering friendship."

Zrebar waved her hand. "May I say something?"

"Of course."

"It's easy to think too much and let your fear of imperfection win. I have put my trust in God on so many occasions. Partha and I lost two of our children—I mean they died, not that we couldn't find them—at different times during our years of fleeing in Iraq and Syria. I would hate to have another family suffer like that."

A stillness descended as people pondered Zrebar's words, measuring their own lives and tribulations against Zrebar's. Shayla let this stillness sit while it remained vital and then spoke before it soured. "I have a piece of paper with a circle in the centre. The circle represents a high level of involvement with refugees. As you leave, could you write your name as close to the centre as represents your own desired level of involvement at this point? This will help us get a better sense of how we as a congregation are feeling about the concrete tasks of supporting the refugees.

"I'll type up and circulate some notes from today so they'll be available for next Sunday's meeting about the Seattle proposal." She grinned. "But I'm not planning to help clean up today. I hope some of you will make that your contribution."

Shayla circulated her notes to the congregation a few days later. They included the page with the circle on it and the names of those who had attended the potluck lunch. The name "Maureen" sat in the middle of the circle, showing she had an interest in taking a central role. Maureen reported a few days later that the page had resulted in several people phoning her to ask confidentially why she wanted to support the initiative. They said they would not be attending the congregational meeting the following Sunday about the proposal from Seattle.

Decision Time

The congregation met in a brown wooden building that looked like a modern interpretation of the traditional church form; it dated from the mid-1990s. A semicircle of lightly upholstered chairs, rather than pews, filled the sanctuary. Natural light radiated through the tall window slits, giving no hint that stained glass had ever been contemplated. The gray commercial carpet somehow managed to harmonize with walls of what the paint chip called "desert sage." The ambiance was warm, if slightly functional.

After All Saints' Sunday service and following coffee and chatting in the rectangular foyer, about two dozen people drifted back into the left corner of the sanctuary, close to the audio control board. Nobody knew why the first person had chosen to sit in that particular area but everyone else had followed. They waited patiently for the meeting to begin.

Not everyone expected at the meeting had yet arrived from their socializing and washroom visits. Even after many years, the congregation had yet to develop an intuitive sense of how soon after the service another activity should begin.

Since it seemed disrespectful to make those who were present wait even longer, Pastor Ellen decided to start but to keep the agenda light until everyone arrived.

The weekly church bulletin had described the meeting as an opportunity to talk about the previous Sunday's lunch discussion and begin deciding whether to partner with the Seattle congregation. An announcement during the service had emphasized that agreeing to sponsor would require some individuals to form a group to support the family for at least a year. A vague "we should do this" from the congregation was less compelling for those on the elected church council than the personal commitment of "I will indeed help do the work."

Standing in front of the group, the cordless microphone almost touching her lips, Ellen began. "Let's start by reflecting on last week's potluck. What went well? What might we want to do differently next time? You don't have to say anything profound. Just what caught your attention."

There was silence as people thought. A little too much silence perhaps, as if people were uncomfortable frankly expressing their views now before the congregation.

Finally, Paul rose and spoke tentatively, "Well, to say something superficial—"

"Superficial works," Ellen interjected. "I'm going to ask everyone to use the mike because while people in front of you can probably hear you, it can be hard for those behind you."

Paul waited to receive a cordless microphone and then fumbled to see if it was turned on. "The potluck felt kind of chaotic and unorganized at the beginning." Ellen privately agreed, but her heart sank nonetheless. Might this criticism be an indication of some current of discontent or unease she had not previously detected?

Paul continued. "But as time passed, we seemed to find our rhythm. It ended up being a really good session, but the beginning felt rocky to me."

This was not where Ellen had thought he would go, although she was pleased that he did. Her surprise made her feel less confident about accurately assessing the mood of the meeting. "Other comments?" she asked.

Again silence, perhaps a thoughtful silence, but it nevertheless threw Ellen off balance. It seemed out of character for those present, all of whom she viewed as dedicated, open people.

"I'm very aware that sometimes, if there's a strong feeling in a meeting, if you happen to think differently than others, it can be hard to voice your opinion," she said gently. "If that's your situation,

I want to encourage you to speak up because part of being a community and working towards consensus is that everybody's voice is important. All those voices help us with our discernment. I hope this encourages everyone to feel free to make whatever comments they want to make today."

Ellen followed this with reassurance about the financial side of the proposed sponsorship.

"Let me bring you up to speed on Seattle. The congregation is currently sorting out the route their money will take because they have to be very careful about legal considerations on both sides of the border. Charitable donations can't be sent directly to particular refugees because governments want to ensure there aren't side arrangements that divert money or reward middlemen with kickbacks. It has to be a general gift to a legitimate organization, such as our relief and development agency. The Americans will have to simply trust that we in Canada will use their un-earmarked donation, if that's a word, in a way that meets our mutual intent."

I'm brilliant, thought Ellen. *If money doesn't get people talking, nothing will.*

She then mentioned the variety of ways for refugees to enter Canada. "An advantage of private sponsorship is that it can be faster. There's some evidence that refugees who have specific individuals helping them, rather than government in general, adapt more readily to the new country. But I'm talking too much. What are your questions and comments?"

Corinne, a personable and caring individual, asked a question that was entirely in character. "Do we have details about the family to be sponsored? How many children, for example, and their ages?"

"If all goes as envisioned, it will be a family with two parents and three kids. I think they're fairly young kids."

"It would help to know the ages of the kids," Corrine probed.

"We'll get those details if we decide to move forward," Ellen said. "At this point, we can't have access to personal information because we haven't committed yet. All I've heard through our relief agency is that the kids are younger."

The discussion shifted to relationships with others, the Seattle group in particular. The impression was that the Seattle people wanted some hands-on engagement, perhaps helping with initial house set-up during a work weekend, but recognized that distance would limit their involvement mainly to supporting the project financially. "As for the refugees' sister, who apparently lives just across the river in Surrey," Ellen said, "I hope we can arrange to meet with her quickly."

Shayla spoke for the first time. "Don't forget that the Badawi family is also willing to be involved. Partha is on disability leave, so he has some time."

Faye rose slowly and hooked her cane on the chair in front of her before speaking. She was concerned about living arrangements, especially since Vancouver was one of the most expensive cities in the world for housing. "This is a formidable hurdle. On the other hand, hundreds of thousands of local working people manage to get by somehow."

What would happen if the trust fund is spent faster than expected? Because Canadian Lutheran World Relief (known as CLWR) would disburse the money in monthly installments, the money was guaranteed to last the entire year. The real problem was that the payments would likely be inadequate because the government's minimum requirement was pegged only to income assistance or welfare rates.

Penny, a task oriented person, asked, "What about expenses not covered under the government medical plan? Would the Seattle church help, or would we have to look after them?"

Ellen spoke slowly. "I don't think we should expect Seattle to help with these types of things. I'm not sure what the new government standard is regarding dental coverage, but emergency dental is covered. Routine cleaning and standard fillings may not be. That's the situation in much of the world. People in many countries get dental care when they can afford it. That's not great, but the situation in Canada for refugees might be similar to that. I presume we'd try to help as much as we can, but it's also possible we wouldn't even hear about those issues."

Heather, who worked in social services, was confident she already knew the answer to her question but wanted everyone to have the information. "So after the one year," she said, "is the family eligible for income assistance from the government if they need it?"

"Yes," Ellen said. "After the year, they're considered full Canadian landed immigrants and have access to exactly the same services as everyone else." She corrected herself. "Permanent residents is the current terminology, I think, not landed immigrants."

"So our obligation would be one year financially and then many years of friendship?" Heather asked.

"Yes, for sure about the first year," Ellen responded. "But there's no obligation to be friends after that. When we sponsored refugees in my home congregation years ago, some refugees maintained lasting relationships while others went on to do their own thing. They're free; we don't want to hold them. It's love, pure and simple. Set them free."

"An observation based on my experience," Ricardo interjected. "I'm an immigrant who's been in Canada for seven years. Getting here and the first little while are not the main challenges, although they're significant. It's what happens after. There will be a lot of support needed even after the first year, especially if they don't speak the language. I agree with what's been said about providing just the basics of everyday life, but eventually the kids will want to have what other children at school have."

Others spoke along similar lines, emphasizing that even immigrants who have been here for a long time find it hard to adjust.

"It's a huge shift," Ellen said. "The Badawi family would be the first to say that their life isn't easy, but they're also happy that their kids' lives are better. But I don't think we could ever commit to, say, five years of financial or other support. At some point, we have to trust that the system will work.

"Will that be enough? I think back to Vietnamese boat people in the 1970s. When they arrived, they had absolutely nothing. They arrived on our shores and were dumped into the community. They've gone on to do some pretty amazing things, starting businesses and being successful.

"But that's not to take away from the reality that life will be hard, that they will have less than others, and that the adjustment will be hard. We're not offering them upper-middle-class standing. We'd just be offering subsistence survival while they get their bearings."

Ellen turned her eyes to the ceiling for a moment and then returned her gaze to the crowd. It looked as though families with young children had begun slipping away. "I'd like to go back to something Zrebar said last week. I fear that I may sound like I'm pushing you to decide in favour of sponsoring refugees, but I'm actually just trying to help us keep everything in perspective.

"Zrebar mentioned that when her family arrived in Canada, they didn't feel they had to have everything, that she would have been content to sleep on the floor. Our standards sometimes get in the way when we think we need to do more than the refugees actually expect. They may be thinking, 'My children are safe. We're in a new country. We have a new start. Bottom line: We have a roof over our head, we have food in our stomach, and nobody is shooting at us.' Anything beyond that is gravy, I think.

"Once again, I'm not trying to urge you towards a particular decision because I won't be part of any welcoming committee if you decide to proceed. This is your decision as a congregation. I'm just trying to help you see that sometimes we set standards far beyond what is needed. I'm contrasting subsistence living here with not getting out of where they currently are."

A reflective silence again descended as the group thought about the proposal. The obvious, urgent questions had been posed. What else needed consideration?

It seemed to Ellen that, although not a great deal that was new had emerged, many people had arrived at the meeting with only partial information, and now everyone had as complete a picture as possible at this point. More questions and answers would likely just be variations on a theme. It was time to shift from information sharing to decision making.

Ellen took a long breath. "What do you want to do next? I remind you that this is not my decision. Are you ready to take a straw vote on this? Do you need more time to think? What is the will of God's people at All Saints Church?"

Ellen's questions prompted some stirring. Making a decision could be uncomfortable. Finally a female voice said, "Proceed."

"Does that mean take a vote?" Ellen asked. "If yes, I'd like to propose a secret ballot so that people can be honest. I think that's really important. Feeling pressure is not helpful."

Nobody commented, much less objected, and Ellen took silence to mean consent. "I'll go get some paper. Meanwhile, you can talk about who would need to be part of the support group if the church decides to take on a sponsorship."

As Ellen walked out of the room, Joanna, the chair of the church council, strode to the front.

"Do we have people who are willing to make a commitment if we vote to proceed?" she asked. "I think sponsoring is a great idea, but I personally don't have the time to be involved. It's fine for us to talk in general, but we need people who would commit from the get-go to attend meetings, help the family, and do the work."

"It would be good if people providing support had fairly flexible hours to go to the airport, get them to appointments, and so on," Faye noted.

Paul raised his hand. "On last week's sign-up sheet asking people to place themselves according to how centrally involved they'd like to be, I put my name halfway to the centre. I'm retired, so I'm one of the people who is available in the daytime."

"Judi and I are nearer the centre," Shayla said. "We're not available during the day so we're thankful you're available then."

Paul nodded. "I know Judi's spoken in the past about her immigrant experiences and of learning English in Canada. I think that's part of her interest, a desire to give something back."

Penny spoke next. "I was waffling at first. Yes, I can provide sugar and flour, or write a cheque. That's easy. What's really needed is hard and more like adopting a child. I work in a job that's more than full time, plus I have a pretty new family, so the prospect of committing more time is something I struggle with. Yet I believe with all my heart this is something I need to be involved in. So I'm not at the centre of the circle, but I'm close."

A number of side conversations developed as Pastor Ellen returned and distributed slips of paper. "Please don't write anything yet," she said. "We need to be clear about the question. How about this? 'Shall we sponsor a Syrian refugee family, provided the Seattle group comes through with the money that's needed? Yes or no.' Is everybody good with that?

"I was asked earlier today if there could be proxy votes if we got as far as voting today. I said I would ask you, but I've changed my mind. I'm just going to rule no, that people have to be here to vote. Upon reflection, this seems the fairest way because there could be other people who would have given a proxy if they had known about that option. Plus, those not here might be operating under incomplete or inaccurate information."

Ellen waited to be questioned or challenged. Nothing happened. She waited a few more seconds and then repeated the question for the ballot.

It didn't take long for each person to write yes or no.

"Thanks for your time," Ellen said. "This meeting was longer than I expected, but I think it was constructive and worthwhile. If you want to wait for the results, let's get two people to quickly count the ballots. Could I have two volunteers?"

Ellen scanned the room and found two hands partially raised. "Carol and Dave, thanks." The two scrutineers collected the ballots and crossed the sanctuary to place them on the lid of the baby grand piano. They sorted the ballots into two piles, then counted and recounted each pile.

They returned to the meeting and Dave took the microphone. "Twenty-five yes and three no."

Ellen remained neutral. "The next step will be to inform the rest of the congregation, and then church council will have to make an official motion. They'll take your feedback today as an important part of their decision making. We're a community that values consensus. Thanks everyone."

Several days later, Pastor Ellen still couldn't shake the unease she'd experienced at the beginning of Sunday's meeting. Despite the weeks of informal conversation, perhaps things were moving too fast for people who were new to the refugee issue. She worried she had missed an undercurrent of opposition. The occasional "What about the homeless people who are already here? Shouldn't we be doing more for them, rather than importing more problems?" and "Why do we care more about other countries than our own impoverished Indigenous communities?" led her to conclude that an abundance of caution might be a good strategy.

A bit of backtracking, as humbling as it might be, was probably prudent. Ellen reached for her computer and composed a message for the weekly email of church announcements. She recapped the issue and what had happened the previous Sunday, and then wrote:

"Upon reflection, I've come to think this refugee decision would best be made at a formal meeting of the congregation under council's chairing, rather than relying on last week's casual gathering, and then

19

a decision at a council meeting, even though we don't technically need a congregational meeting because we wouldn't be committing any of our own money. So there will be a special meeting of all baptized members on Sunday April 10, right after worship. Please plan to attend! This invitation includes adherents because we'd like to hear your thoughts, even though you're not eligible to vote."

Two days after the message went out, Ellen, pressed for time, ate lunch at her desk. *Where did people get the idea that clergy simply filled their weekdays with leisurely prayer, careful sermon preparation, and the occasional pastoral visit?* Her first meeting with Karl Golds seemed a century ago. She felt bad that he and the Syrian Refugee Action Group were still waiting for All Saints to make up its mind about the partnership. On top of this, another delay had just come up as bureaucrats scrambled to administer politicians' policy modifications midstream.

Once again, she composed an email she would have preferred not to send.

"Karl, this is just a quick note to let you know we are in a bit of a holding pattern. CLWR cannot move forward until the government assigns numbers to each of the private sponsorship groups. The government apparently has some sort of a quota system they're now sorting through. So all the work by the agencies for private sponsorship is on hold. Hopefully we'll hear more soon."

When the congregation met after church on April 10 to make a formal decision, Ellen was both delighted that it was so anticlimactic—a non-event, really—and perplexed that her disquiet was apparently unfounded. The turnout was modest but consistent with business meetings on other topics. A few questions were posed on familiar topics and then people were ready to vote: thirty-eight for (provided, of course, that funding was in place from Seattle) and five against. Meeting adjourned.

Official Launch

Ten long months after the Kurdi family's tragedy spurred William and Karl to action, the American and Canadian partnership to help Syrian refugees was finally launched. Mount Olivet dispatched the first installment of funds for deposit with Canadian Lutheran World Relief, followed shortly by All Saints signing the legal undertaking to sponsor a refugee family under the auspices of CLWR.

Here are the key emails documenting how the joint initiative was formalized. The first messages concerned the transfer of funds, followed by other emails with news that CLWR had officially designated a particular Syrian family to be sponsored.

Pastor Ellen first acknowledged she'd received a cheque from Seattle and then passed the information on to CLWR:

July 12, 2016
Pastor Ellen to Syrian Refugee Action Group:

> Our church chairperson, Joanna, and I picked up your cheque yesterday. I'm sending another email off to Noor at Canadian Lutheran World Relief to see if the paperwork is ready. When all is prepared, two people from our group will sign the paperwork and deposit the cheque with CLWR.
>
> I'll be away for three weeks of vacation, but Joanna will look after communications. Also we will want to get things planned for your visit at the end of August, if those dates, August 27 and 28, are still in the works.
>
> With thanks to God for all of you as we begin this great adventure!

Noor from CLWR to Pastor Ellen:

We are working on the documents. Some information is missing. As soon as we receive it, the papers will be ready for submission to the federal government.

Now that the months of talking were bearing fruit, the parties were eager to get to know each other better. Pastor Ellen was still the only Canadian partner anyone from SRAG had met in person.

July 13, 2016
Karl in Seattle to All Saints:

> It is so nice to make your acquaintance. I am very excited to meet you and pursue this partnership. Let's confirm a visit to your church on August 27–28; I'll get you a final count as the date approaches.

> In the meantime, please send an update as soon as you meet with CLWR. If you learn anything about the family(ies) assigned to us, we can launch the final fundraising push. And if you gain an insight re: potential timing, please advise. (I know this is highly unpredictable and we understand that any estimates are fraught with potential error.)

Greg, a staff member at Mount Olivet, to All Saints:

> And just so everyone is also aware, we hit $21,000 this past weekend with another larger donation. I think we'll get the full amount soon! Blessings.

Just a week later, word came from the Canadian Lutheran World Relief that a family had been officially identified for sponsorship. "The envelope please." Drum roll. "And the winner is…"

July 21, 2016
Noor to All Saints:

It is my pleasure to inform you that a Syrian family of five has been identified. The forms have been completed. This refugee family has suffered not only from the horrors of war in Syria but also from religious persecution—as a religious minority belonging to the Christian faith. They are currently in Lebanon. They have a close relative living in Surrey to assist in initial settlement assistance together with folks from All Saints Lutheran Church.

You are welcome to come to the office anytime next week to sign the papers and drop the cheque as well. Please let us know which day will suit you. We will need your contact information and your date of birth to complete the *Undertaking* form. You could also complete the *Sponsor Assessment* form when you come to our office.

Joanna to Noor:

Thanks! I faxed my personal info to the CLWR office. What hours are you available next week? 9 to 5 or evenings too? I need to find someone on the committee to come with me and most aren't as available as I am.

Noor to Joanna:

One person will be enough to sign the papers and make them ready for submission. So, please let us know when you will be coming. The office is closed on Fridays during the summer.

KEY PLAYERS

Visitors from the South

The plan was simple. The visitors from Mount Olivet would arrive late Saturday afternoon for a potluck dinner hosted by All Saints. Following the evening program, they would divide into family groupings for bed and breakfast in a handful of homes. They would return with their All Saints hosts for Sunday morning worship and then depart for Seattle after a lunch at the church.

Before recounting this event, let's step back in time to the first meeting of the All Saints Refugee Welcoming Team. It had been scheduled for August 5 upon the uncomfortable realization that nobody had any idea what All Saints was going to do when the SRAG group arrived in just a few weeks' time. This meeting confirmed who would become the core members of the team.

Paul notified the other five members that he would be away on a tenting road trip. Judi, on the other hand, attended the meeting and was horrified to learn that her enthusiasm had been taken by some to mean that she'd volunteered to chair the committee and oversee organizational matters. After clarifying the ways in which she was and was not willing to be involved, she agreed to supervise the arrangements for the Saturday evening dinner and program.

A couple of days after the meeting, Judi texted Paul. "Hope you are back in town. Reason I'm messaging you is because the Seattle group will come to see us on August 27. Can you be the host of the

25

evening meeting? The group thinks you are the best person to do this. Don't say no to me, please!"

Paul replied with a tentative yes. "I expect to be home Friday, so we can talk soon and you can help me understand this better."

Judi and Paul did indeed talk the following Sunday and developed an agenda for the Saturday evening program. "Does it really have to be this long?" Judi asked incredulously.

"If you can find something we can omit, I'd be happy to do it," Paul replied. "I'm not seeing anything, though. There's a good rationale for everything."

AGENDA

Welcome and Introduction
> Opening prayer and group singing
> Confirmation of agenda
> Description of All Saints church for the Seattle visitors
>> Introduction of welcoming team members
> Description of Mount Olivet, Seattle church
>> Introduction of Syrian Refugee Action Group (SRAG) members

Developments to Date
> How All Saints came to sponsor an Iraqi family several years ago
> Mount Olivet's interest in Syrian refugees and US barriers they encountered
> How Mount Olivet connected with All Saints
>> Role of Canadian Lutheran World Relief (CLWR)
> Mount Olivet's fundraising
> Our Syrian family and where things now stand

Broader Context (three short PowerPoint presentations)
> Syria
> Cross-cultural considerations

Canadian government refugee process

Interactions and Communications between All Saints
and SRAG
   Aspirations and protocols

Planning for the Family's Arrival
   Government and CLWR processes
   Anticipated timeline
   Housing: short and long term
   Furnishings

Outstanding Questions and Next Steps

Tonight and Sunday
   Billets for homestay
   Information to be presented during service to congregation
   Enhanced coffee time/potluck lunch on Sunday

Adjournment
   Singing

Two weeks later, the Mount Olivet contingent arrived on schedule, some having rendezvoused north of Seattle, near Everett, to carpool. A few had spent Saturday afternoon shopping in Vancouver while the rest explored the trails and pedestrian suspension bridge in Lynn Canyon Park in the mountains of North Vancouver. Most of the Badawi family attended the evening. To the pleasant surprise of the members of All Saints, they brought two visiting relatives—Partha's father from Australia and his aunt from Chicago. Along with their friends, the Qatabs from Syria, the ten newcomers from the Middle East provided an air of authenticity and wider partnership to the evening.

Judi arranged a simple icebreaker to encourage conversation among strangers. As people entered the church, she gave each person three sticky dots to place on their chest next to their name tag. The game's objective was to collect as many dots as possible by tricking others into saying the word "yes" when they expressed agreement. People mingled warmly and then, when it was time for the meal to begin, they sat around a single large table composed of many smaller tables pushed together. Food platters were passed from one person to another, family style, in random order.

Three dozen chairs in the sanctuary formed a tight horseshoe facing the projection screen in the front right corner. The simple physical act of walking from the dinner table into the sanctuary set the tone for the more formal portion of the evening—except for the teens and young children, who disappeared in the opposite direction in search of more interesting things to do than sitting through a meeting.

The prayer Paul used to open the session drew upon phrases and language found in the Koran but remained entirely within the bounds of mainline Christianity. He began. "Let's ask God to bless this part of the evening, using a prayer that I hope is inclusive, or at least respectful, of the various faith traditions among us."

Gracious God,
We come before you with praise in our hearts,
    for you are the merciful lord of the worlds
        and master of the judgment day.
It is you whom we worship
    and to whom we call for help.
We ask you to guide us on paths that you have blessed.

These paths are ones that we cannot always find on our own
    and which sometimes surprise us.
Over two thousand years ago, a conquered and suffering people
    prayed to you for a deliverer
    and you sent Jesus into the world.

His message of love and justice was not quite what was expected,
and even today we still sometimes misunderstand His words
and actions.
We need your guidance and support to live up
to what Jesus and the prophets have called us to be.

In our own century, we thank you for the gift of the
Badawi family,
who you have brought into our lives.
We had no idea that this is what you had planned for us,
yet they have become a doorway through which we
are learning
how to see your compassion and activity in cultures
and places
that are far away from where we currently live.

And now you are setting us on yet another path,
one on which you have given us unexpected companions
from Seattle
to encourage and enable us,
a path on which we will make new friends
from yet another troubled part of the world.
We pray that you would give us wisdom and patience on
this journey,
compassion and forgiveness,
and joy in seeing your hand at work
in ways and in places we had not previously noticed.

We give you thanks and praise, most generous and
merciful God.
Amen.

Shayla stepped forward with her guitar to lead a couple of songs
about friends and fellowship. Many of the items on the program
communicated information some people already knew, but they

were meant to ensure everybody had the same information about the developments to date. The three slide presentations, however, showed what was new information for many—namely, general material about Syria and refugee sponsorship.

The first presentation was half a dozen slides about Syria, a country roughly the size of Washington State but with two and a half times the population (if you include citizens currently displaced in other countries). Three quarters of Syrians are Sunni Muslims. Shia Muslims (thirteen percent) are a little more prevalent than Orthodox and Catholic Christians (ten percent). Almost one third of the Christian population, around half a million people, have fled their homes.

Syria's modern history has been harsh. The Ottoman Turks occupied the territory until the French took over under an international mandate at the end of World War I. The country gained independence in 1946 but a series of half a dozen coups began in 1949. Since 1970, it's been governed under a non-democratic presidency, with the uprisings of 2011 against the current government leading to outright civil war.

The second presentation highlighted the issue of cultural sensitivity with Syrians. For example, because of limited physical contact between the sexes in public settings, when men are introduced to women, they should normally let the woman take the initiative in extending her hand. If she chooses not to shake hands, then the polite greeting is for the man to nod with one hand on his chest.

Loud and animated conversation is common, yet opinions are often expressed indirectly. Eye contact is direct, and raised eyebrows with a slight backward flick of the head means "no." Punctuality is not valued, and Syrians are generous with giving their time to others. Important decisions should be made slowly, and bartering is expected.

Views about gender issues vary across religious and secular groups, but public displays of affection and homosexuality are taboo. Holding hands within the sexes, however, is simply viewed as acceptable friendship.

The third presentation provided highlights from a Canadian government presentation on refugee resettlement that Joanna, the chair of All Saints' church council, had attended. It emphasized that, although sponsors have a great many specific tasks to accomplish for and with refugees, their most important role is to empower newcomers and foster their ability to live independently. It described the cultural shock many involuntary immigrants experience as a long process involving an initial honeymoon that typically gives way to a personal crisis, in light of the challenges of settling in a new land. Eventually the newcomers gain a new worldview and change their self-identity, which leads to an acceptance of their new life.

Questions and comments increasingly punctuated the presentations. By the end of the third presentation, Paul decided the conversation was taking on a healthy life of its own. He largely jettisoned the rest of the agenda after a bathroom-and-stretch break that also gave the observant Muslims a few minutes to discretely disappear into a side room for their evening prayers. Paul's role as facilitator switched from managing a list of tasks to promoting relationships by simply ensuring a microphone was passed to all who had something to say before the evening ended.

The All Saints hosts and Mount Olivet guests drifted into church the following morning, a few drowsy from a late night of chatting over red wine. At the other end of the energy spectrum, two men had jogged seven kilometers through the wetlands portion of a local park, followed by an uphill slog to shower and breakfast at their townhouse. All the visitors were introduced during the service and given the opportunity to say a few words. Following a lunch consisting partly of leftovers from the previous evening, the Seattle crew waved goodbye and slowly exited the parking lot.

Metamorphosis

The All Saints hosts were still thinking about the visit from Mount Olivet three weeks later. Something remarkable had occurred that weekend, but their thoughts as they folded laundry and walked dogs remained vague. Without discussing their impressions with others, it was hard to give shape to their feelings, much less grasp how they were coming to see the world, and their place in it, in new ways.

Half a dozen people settled into Vicki's living room, comfortable on the sofas and with each other. Nibbles and beverages were served, and the conversation drifted to the visit from Seattle.

"The guests from Mount Olivet were incredibly friendly," Shayla said. "I'm glad the visit went well because, if we can't figure out how to host a few of our neighbours from across the border for even a single night, how can we welcome refugees for their entire lives? It's like I needed proof of our ability to be hospitable, with everybody coming through and doing their tasks. The visit showed me we really can welcome strangers, doing it well and enjoying it."

"I'm laughing," Penny jumped in, "because when I asked my son if it was okay for somebody to stay in his room while he and my husband were away, a puzzled look crossed my husband's face. He said, 'For some reason, I thought you knew this person.' 'Well, no, I don't,' I replied, 'although it won't be a random stranger.' He fixated on an unknown person coming into our home while I was alone. 'Honey,' I said, 'they're Lutheran. They'll be fine.' He remained horrified."

The doorbell rang and Vicki dashed downstairs. A moment later, Pastor Ellen slipped into the room. "Sorry I'm late." She settled on a padded upright chair next to the couch and continued. "I want to say that you were absolutely amazing when Seattle came. I know I've already said that a couple of times in other situations, but I can't say it enough." She paused and spoke more thoughtfully. "Something shifted in the way All Saints functions that night."

"Yes," Penny said, re-entering the conversation, "I wonder if the Spirit was at work on Saturday night when our first refugee family from Iraq, the Badawi family, and their friends, the Qatabs, arrived for dinner. The eyes of some of the Seattle people opened wide. For all I know, they may never have spoken to anybody in a hijab before."

"Oh, I think they have," Vicki replied with a slight grin. "The teacher who stayed with me had Muslim kids in his classes. He talked about his school finding a place for them to pray and what happened when it was during class time."

Pastor Ellen summed up. "I do think it was an act of God, frankly, for all of us. The learning experience, the richness of the evening, the relationship building, the rubbing shoulders."

Judi rose and walked to the dining room. She returned with a bowl of Coronation grapes in one hand and a platter of squares in the other. "Moon cake," she explained as she served Penny and Shayla. "It's a treat from the Chinese bakery, but not everyone has a Chinese palate. Try a small piece and see if you like it." After some small talk about bakeries and sushi, the discussion turned to cultural differences.

"One of the differences between the United States and Canada is that the US tends not to celebrate ethnic identities to the same degree as us. You're an American first. That's expected to be your primary identity as you leave other cultural pieces behind. That's hard for immigrants, but it has pluses and minuses. So this idea of allowing people to be who they are, of allowing another culture to enrich your own, asking what we can learn from what some might call a clan or family mentality, it's probably quite a bit about how you can love and care for other people."

"The PowerPoint slide that said homosexuality is taboo in much of the Middle East really hit me. Some of our visitors are embracing a lifestyle that's absolutely forbidden in Syrian culture, yet they are the ones showing kindness and compassion to bring Syrians to safety. I think it's incredibly selfless. The Mount Olivet people are totally doing the Good Samaritan thing. And they don't just want to give money. They want to be involved."

"I have to say I cringed when I saw that slide."

"If that taboo is the reality, we have to acknowledge it. Likewise, I had worried how the Badawis might react that evening. I didn't know if they had ever spoken to an American who wasn't ready to shoot them. It turned out that their aunt lives in Chicago, so it was no big deal, but we have to be sensitive to what could potentially have been a problem."

Shayla shook her head, frowning. "Yes, it was a big deal. The Badawis have had such traumatic experiences, and their feelings towards Americans have been beyond bad. Their kids still have flashbacks, and yet their aunt lives in America. Their family is progressive and well educated. Zrebar's dad has been all over the world with his psychology background. But their personal experiences with Americans since 9/11 have been only bad. Our evening was the first time they've had a meal with someone from the US."

"One of the things we did, God did, was to create was a safe space, a peaceful meeting ground."

"Maintaining a safe space is going to be critical for our stressed family and even our diverse set of sponsors. Sometimes it's just tiny things, a tipping point, that cause blows ups. If we we're not prepared, we'll overreact."

"Talking about little things, I hadn't given any thought as to what clothing might be appropriate. My dress was rather short and I became very self-conscious. There was lots of boundary testing and culture touching that evening."

"We're going to have to pay a lot of attention to cultural practices and expectations. In Toronto, a Muslim dad wanted his kids excused from music lessons in public school. The school made all sorts of accommodations. The kids didn't have to sing, they didn't have to stand up for 'O Canada,' but they had to be in music class. I'm a musician, but I've never talked to the Badawis about the role music plays in their faith. Is it sometimes not allowed?"

"Some differences could seem unimportant to us, but they might not be something that the refugees can lightly say, 'Oh, things are different in Canada. We'll just accept it.' We have to be aware of ingrained attitudes so that we can intervene graciously if needed."

The exuberance at the beginning of the evening had shifted to a more nuanced consideration of the challenges that refugee sponsorship would entail. "Partha Badawi said," came a comment from the corner, "that when he first came to Canada and met Pastor ET, he had never been in a church before. He reported his meeting back home and everybody said, 'Beware. They'll try to convert you. Christians are not to be trusted.'"

Several bodies tensed. "Do other cultures really see us as untrustworthy?"

"Yeah, for sure. Haven't you ever launched into an engaging, reciprocal conversation only to discover that the other person was just a Christian salesperson with an agenda? Some churches even teach their members how to do this charade in evangelism classes."

"And there's more. This conservative Syrian-Christian family that we'll be welcoming may arrive with a set of biases about us and about Muslims. It could even be hatred towards the Muslims, perhaps violent hatred, though probably not. It's hard for me to say this, but my own experience has been that the prejudice of Christians is greater than that of the average Muslim. The Muslims soften when they see we're not trying to convert or exploit them. Christians towards Muslims can be different."

"By way of an update," Pastor Ellen said, attempting to lighten the mood without changing the topic of cultural perspectives, "our visitors spoke in their church this past Sunday about their visit to Canada. It's a big deal for some in the Mount Olivet congregation because, in some ways, everything revolves around America. In their minds, it can be a big trip to come up here."

"Isn't that something?"

"Well, crossing the border is a big deal for me, too. I haven't been to the United States forever."

Ellen continued. "They were amazed at the beauty of our area. 'Gorgeous,' they said. They hadn't been sure what they were coming to."

"Americans may know Vancouver, but there's no reason for them to know the suburbs."

"They had a very good time here. I'm told people back at Mount Olivet were in tears when they heard the weekend report. They think All Saints is amazing."

The room filled with laughter. "Prolong the honeymoon as long as possible, because I would have said we suck. We don't even have a name for our refugee group. Have we settled on the 'welcoming team'?"

"I felt so tiny and overwhelmed. They're the competent group."

"That's the thing with a mutual relationship. They went home saying, 'We're so inspired by you. You're a terrific community.' And we felt that way about them."

"Well, at least the last part is true."

"That's the beauty of mutuality. We get to see ourselves through the eyes of others and ask ourselves if, deep down, isn't that who we really are? Absolutely, that's the real us. And we're now going to get called by God to grow into that."

Broadening Horizons

Sponsoring refugees entails much more than simply learning how to meet the living needs of newcomers. Sponsors are exposed to a constellation of networks and service providers that opens their minds to the plight of displaced people. Here is a sampling of the conversations at All Saints during September.

Kurdi Family Update

The father of Alan Kurdi, the drowned toddler, had initially wanted to come not just anywhere in Canada but specifically to a sister, Tima, who lived a mere fifteen minutes from All Saints church. When the Kurdis abandoned this dream because of bureaucratic barriers imposed by the previous Canadian government, their destination shifted to the more welcoming Germany, where some relatives had already arrived safely. It was during a clandestine four-mile crossing from the Turkish mainland to the Greek island of Kos, the first step in an arduous route through central Europe for desperate asylum seekers, that the tiny craft capsized in a notoriously windy portion of the Aegean Sea.

Vicki discovered that she had an indirect connection with the Kurdis. "Sometimes good things come, even from Facebook," she said with a twinkle. "Do you remember the group photo when the Mount Olivet people and the Badawi group came to supper that evening at the end of August? Well, I 'liked' the photo and it must have gone on the newsfeed because it reached my friend Wendy. We went to Europe together in our early twenties, but I hadn't seen her for ages. 'I see you're involved with sponsoring,' she messaged me. 'I'm a sponsor. Do you want to get together and catch up?'

"So she and I went for dinner last week. It was interesting to meet someone with firsthand experience sponsoring a Syrian family. But it wasn't just any family. The dad is a brother of Tima Kurdi and an uncle of the little boy on the beach."

"No way!" Judi exclaimed.

"Yes," Vicki replied. "Five neighbours in a cul-de-sac got together and became sponsors under the government's small group provisions. You know, it's one of the other types of sponsorships besides government sponsorships and the kind of private sponsorship we're involved in. And who else lives on that little street? Tima Kurdi. The brother and his family moved in with her."

"So the sponsors lived pretty much next door to their Syrian family?" Bruce asked.

"Yes, it was a huge convenience to be close by. Wendy ended up doing things like helping the kids with school and homework. Plus, Tima could help so much with language and the transition to Canada. Of course, she wasn't available all the time.

"The brother and his family arrived in December in sandals," Vicki continued. "Nobody was around the next afternoon to translate. Wendy popped the parents and five kids into her van to get proper winter shoes. Nobody speaking any English, but she just went to the store with them, figuring out how to get shoes for all of them. She says you just kind of jump in and do what needs to be done."

Bruce searched his memory about the last article he'd seen in the newspaper on the Kurdis. "I don't think the brother is living in that house any longer, is he? Wasn't the family large?"

"Yes, making the housing cramped and stressful. But it seems to have worked out. After a short time living some distance away, the family found a place close by where the kids can continue in their schools."

Judi noted that the brother was a barber and still looking for work according to an article she'd read.

"Yes," Vicki said. "The problem seems to be that Tima's hairdressing business wasn't doing as well as they'd like. It's located somewhere over on the north side. The brother apparently worried that if he kept working at her shop, he would just take business away from her.

"The wife now has a two-day-a-week job as a dishwasher somewhere in Vancouver. Her English picked way up. Wendy asked her, 'How come you're now able to speak to me?' I guess the wife was listening while she was washing dishes."

"I can't believe how small the world is," Bruce said, circling back to the beginning of the conversation. "Or at least how significant connections get made in our big world. Of all the groups in Canada that the Seattle church could have teamed up with, they've ended up with partners who have indirect connections to the family in the global press that sparked Seattle's involvement in the first place."

Privacy and the Safety of Refugee Relatives
No confidentiality problems had emerged and Pastor Ellen wanted to keep it that way. She gathered the welcoming team together to impress on them the importance of being cautious in their public communications. "Loose lips sink ships," the propaganda posters of World War II had proclaimed.

"It sounds like our family is relatively safe right now as Christians because they're currently in Lebanon," Ellen said. "For either Christian or Muslim refugees, their families in the home country can be punished just because western Christians are helping out. That may seem obvious when Christians are helping Muslims to flee, but even when Christians help Christians to leave, as we are, Christian family members back home can still suffer because they tend to get persecuted in any event. We just provide one more excuse, one more provocation.

"But," she said, "I think our family is probably low risk. I'm actually more concerned about the Badawis because they still have some relatives in Iraq. The Badawis say they're not worried about being associated with us, but I'm uneasy about their situation. I hope I'm wrong.

"If we take photos, we have to be careful about faces and what we post publicly, and be especially vigilant not to tag names. When we write about people, we can use first names or family names, but not both at any one time. This just adds a slight layer, not a lot, but enough to provide a bit more security.

"I know this sounds like conspiracy theory, but a few years ago, we had an isolated case of a couple of Iranians rotating through our local churches to see if any Iranians were worshipping with

Christians. This could result in punishment for families back in Iran by the more extreme sects or punishment for Canadian residents if they return to Iran. I came to recognize a woman who occasionally visited our church. She stopped when we pointed her out publicly and said that surveillance was not acceptable behaviour."

Shayla spoke up. "I know some Iranians who converted to Christianity back in Iran before becoming refugees. They never connect with local Iranians here in Canada, even secular ones. It's a shame, because my few acquaintances with a Persian background are lovely people."

Cultural Sensitivity
Penny squirmed. "I agree with all you're saying about the need to be culturally sensitive, but let's not get carried away or too politically correct. At my workplace, we have Muslims and Sikhs and Jews and Christians, and who knows what else. We even have a Jehovah's Witness who answers the phone when we have parties because he won't participate in anything. At work, we're just people. We're just workers. The Muslims eat when the Sikhs bring Indian food during a festival. The Sikhs and the Hindus, it's all a mishmash. It turns out fine.

"The Muslim ladies take their head scarves off when they come into work, even though Muslim men are present. When they leave the building, they put their scarves back on. After 9/11, we brought everybody into the boardroom and said, 'We're like the United Nations here. Behind these walls at work, we are safe. We respect each other and we work with each other. We do good things with each other.'"

A young man asked, "But does it really go that smoothly when the religious holidays roll around?"

Penny looked at her audience; their body language seemed open. She pitched her voice lower. "In December, we have a Christmas party where everybody dresses up. They wear their Punjabi suits.

We go to an Indian restaurant, of all places, and have a Christmas party. I ask if it's okay that we're celebrating Christmas and they say, 'Of course.' For them, it may be mainly about Santa, but Jesus also has a role in some of their religions as a prophet.

"The Syrian fellows that we just hired are very devout. They wanted to go to prayers on Friday afternoons, but how do you go to your brand new boss and say, 'Oh, by the way, can I have Friday afternoon off?' But Abduhl, an employee, has been going to prayers for twenty-three years. That's just what we do. The newcomers were very timid about going to their female boss to ask if they could perhaps, maybe, on occasion, once in a while, you know, go to prayers. And Monica said, 'Absolutely. Go with Abduhl. Every Friday you can carpool.'

"Everything we do is an opportunity for us to get to know everybody better. I don't think we need to be super worried. We're in Canada, and newcomers recognize that. We have the opportunity to amaze people."

"But isn't that God out ahead doing the stuff, and we're catching up?" a church council member asked.

"Yes, and I have experienced it first hand for twenty years."

Doors to New Lives
Judi was curious. "At the beginning, we expected to get a non-Christian family, probably Muslim. How did we end up with Christians?"

"CLWR made the choice from a pool of refugee applicants, all with equally high needs, regardless of faith," Pastor Ellen replied. "It's usually just a bingo game as to who gets picked. Unless something special happens, which it did in our case.

"Here's my understanding of what happened. The Canadian government recognizes how hard it is for our permanent residents if part of their family remains in danger abroad. So churches are being encouraged to help with what is almost a family reunification plan. When someone in Canada, the sister in Surrey in our case, approaches CLWR to identify individuals they want brought to Canada, CLWR then has a basis to select a particular family from the applicant pool; no one has priority over anyone else at that point. Our family is not jumping a queue."

"How do the Badawis feel about this?" Shayla probed.

"I talked to them about it. They're okay. 'We will help them settle,' they said."

"That is marvellously gracious. Muslims who themselves do not have it easy in Canada are willing to help Christians from another land settle in Canada," Penny commented. "And they may even have their own family members who want to come to Canada but can't get in, for all I know."

Ellen added, "Partha's comment was 'We have left all that strife behind us. This is here; this is now. We are people of faith. We are all people of faith.' I'm trying to remember all the things he said, but his basic message was that he's not going to let discord and hatred rule him in his new land. He left that behind. He says, 'That way of thinking destroyed my life and the lives of so many people. I'm not going to carry that here.'"

"Wow!" exclaimed Penny. "That's really open minded."

"Partha is holding to his beliefs, but it's challenging for him. It challenges him all the time," Ellen said. "Going back to a question a few days ago about having a skimpy skirt or wondering whether it's fine to wear shorts, I'm going to say, not in a militant way, that we just need to be who we are. We make accommodation as best we can, but we can't completely change because part of our role as sponsors is to help refugees find a way to accept us for who we are— as we are doing for them. We're not asking them to change their faith or do things differently. I always get a conversion offer when I go to a Muslim official event. Somebody is always trying to convert me, but I'm not going to do that to them, no matter what.

"I suspect our new family is going to present some challenges for us. We need to know more about the Orthodox community here. Some in that region of the world have been tormented so severely for generations, centuries really, that a distrust of Muslims can be deep-seated. But I think the Badawis are up to the challenge, and I think we are, too.

"I know I'm getting off topic, but Tamas Qatab has been asking me a lot of questions. I would eventually see him becoming an imam, a worship leader. He's very interested in faith. He's the one who went into seclusion after Ramadan, the month of fasting. Somebody goes into seclusion, and he's the one who did it for his community. He's being true to his faith while walking alongside us as Christians, and it's opening his mind. It's opening all our minds.

"What I'm trying to say is that there's something much bigger going on here. It has all these threads."

Learning the Hard Way
The discussion turned to what could be learned from All Saints' first experience of sponsoring refugees almost four years ago. We had been novices and all had not gone as well as we would have liked.

"I think one of the pieces that eroded Annie and William, the most involved of our welcoming group back then, was rubbing the differences so hard," Pastor Ellen said cryptically. "Being the ones to see the newcomers all the time jaded them a little, I think. Wondering if these immigrants would ever be able to fully adapt."

Shayla sighed. "I thought that if Annie had been present last month, she would have been so pleased to hear Partha say, 'Language lessons are crucial for your advancement. Don't think about finding a job first. Do your language improvement and you will find a better job. Maybe I wouldn't have had an accident at work if I had better understood the safety precautions.' That was one of Annie and Will's beefs. Partha just couldn't understand for a long time the importance of language classes. But that's part of the learning."

"It's poignant for sure," Ellen said softly. "The Neufelds wanted to do it right as sponsors, super right, but the Badawis needed to make their own learning experiences."

"You have to make a few errors along the way," Vicki agreed. "That's how we learn. But it's painful."

"There's another lesson for us," Shayla said. "It seems the Neufelds didn't have anybody they could fall back on, or they chose not to fall back on anyone. I don't know what the situation was, but they seemed to feel they were responsible for everything."

Ellen nodded in agreement. "Let's remember that in our work so that it doesn't happen again. You think you can do it but you burn out, only to find you can't then exit graciously. It's a well-patterned behaviour here at All Saints that's played out tragically on several occasions."

"Sometimes you need fallow time," Penny concluded. "I grew up in the church and when I got to university, I became super involved in the church. I thought that's just what you do if you're part of a church. I got so burned out that, when I moved to Vancouver, I needed some time to just be rather than serve on every committee. That was the first time I was actually able to say no, and I took perverse pleasure in doing so."

British Columbia is Better Prepared

Vicki waved the newspaper clipping. "Did anybody else see this article in the September 7 edition of the *Vancouver Sun*? It's about BC now being better prepared for the next wave of Syrian refugees? There's supposed to be 1,500 government-assisted refugees from the Middle East coming to our province before the end of next year, plus 750 privately sponsored ones."

"Was that the one where somebody from the Immigrant Services Society said they now have a well-oiled machine? And that instead of chartered planeloads of refugees arriving all at once, they'll dribble in on commercial flights to spread out the reception work-load? The article I saw was really good."

"Yes. Listen to what it says about some of the orientations given by the BC Muslim Association." Vicki pushed her reading glasses off her head and onto her nose. "He said his Arabic-speaking members are poised to help newcomers handle the inevitable culture shock and adapt to Canadian laws and social customs. Men in particular are being advised to not smoke in public places, not shout even if it's normal and culturally acceptable in their homelands, not hit spouses or children, and not leer at or whisper when they see Canadian women in short skirts.

"He said, 'We tell them, you are here in a different country, a different culture, and you have to accept this since you are being provided with safety and a safety net to come here and live and look after your kids. So you have to abide by the rules here in this country. And most of them appreciate that I warn them, but sometimes there are misunderstandings.'"

Becoming a Team

The half dozen people at the core of the All Saints Refugee Welcoming Team gathered at Vicki's house on a Thursday evening. "I like hosting," she said. "I'm happy to have meetings here now that the kids have moved out."

Paul and Penny looked at each other. "We should have carpooled," Penny said, "since we live almost next door to each other. Next time."

The chitchat subsided and people seemed ready to begin. Paul had jotted down some topics he hoped would be covered that evening. "I was mainly thinking about administrative and communication stuff. Once we get ourselves better organized, who else at All Saints will be involved in specific areas? It's frustrating for somebody to volunteer and then be ignored."

"You're not thinking about the same couple I am, are you?" Judi asked.

45

"Maybe," Paul replied but said nothing further on the topic; instead, he elaborated on his list. "That's what was on my mind. Some of you may have other things you want to discuss."

"Have you looked at the sponsorship handbook?" Shayla asked. "There's way too much work for the few of us to do by ourselves. We need task groups with somebody in charge of each. The leader would recruit more people to help with the task."

A suitable agenda eventually emerged. Now everyone waited for somebody to start the discussion or take the role of chair—nobody did. The seconds passed. For some in the room, administration simply was not their strong point. More importantly, they all wanted to set boundaries for their involvement with the welcoming team, their willingness to work within those boundaries notwithstanding. Agreeing to chair tonight might set a precedent that could make it difficult for the chair to protect their boundaries in the future.

Paul blinked first. "I'd be interested in hearing how everybody wants to help out. You've already told us, Shayla, that with work and a busy family life, you'd prefer to concentrate locally. Given your strong relationship with the Badawis, if you could be our liaison with them, that would be a big help.

"As for me," Paul continued, "refugee sponsorship isn't my passion. I do think it's worthwhile, though, and has the potential to strengthen us as a church community. So I'm here more in a support role to help other people do things that matter a great deal to them."

Penny took the cue about sharing interests. "I work, so I can't do a lot of running around during the day, but I can look on Craigslist, try to find stuff, get donations from people—and not just crap. I mean nice things. When I talk to people about the sponsorship, they are super excited that somebody is actually doing something. Then they ask if they can donate something, for example, bedding."

Judi said she liked arranging social events. "Food, decorations."

"That's so not me," Paul said. "It's great having people whose talents complement each other."

Vicki shifted in her chair. "I really don't know what my role will be. I ended up in this accidentally, probably like everyone."

"Your role is hosting our meetings."

"I'll host them all."

Paul turned to Ellen. "Pastor, you started off doing everything, being the only contact person with Seattle. With the project launched, I know you're trying to hand it off to others. Where do you fit in?"

"Well." Ellen explained that she was still half time at All Saints and half with the BC Synod. "I'm feeling the time pinch right now, especially with some congregational visiting I'm not getting done. That's bothering me." But time wasn't the main reason she wanted more of a background role. "I'm already encouraged by the way you're coming together to share the workload. I don't want to be an obstacle to the emergence of teamwork. Incidentally, I thought you did a great job communicating with Seattle, Shayla."

"Paul and I had an email exchange," Shayla said. "I'm happy to keep communicating with Seattle, but I can't be the lead on government or CLWR documentation. That's a huge piece that's beyond me, so Paul said he'd take it on."

"That piece with officialdom is disappearing," Ellen said. "Most of the paperwork is done."

Judi looked puzzled. "But wasn't Karl enquiring about some form he saw on the Government of Canada website that we haven't completed?"

"What Karl was looking for is Schedule 2 with the details about the applicant's request for refugee status," Ellen explained. "It gives the nitty gritty as to why they became refugees. Typically, All Saints would have received it when Joanna signed the papers for us at CLWR. I wasn't there and had assumed the form would come automatically, but it didn't. Joanna, of course, didn't know to ask for it.

"Anyhow, that paper should be coming soon because I've asked Noor for it. It will document whether our family has been shot or tortured, or if they've lost children. It has all kinds of details that we wouldn't want made public about our own lives."

"So from that we can prepare a summary to distribute to All Saints and Mount Olivet?" Vicki asked tentatively.

Ellen tilted her head back and pursed her lips. "I think Karl can have the full document. Actually, both the All Saints welcoming team and SRAG in Seattle could likely see everything, but you shouldn't pass the information along to others. It's confidential information that's relevant only to the people most involved with the family."

After giving a moment for her recommendation to sink it, she continued. "The other confusion seems to be what a settlement plan is. That's really just a checklist asking 'Have you thought about all the things you need to do when the refugees arrive?' It's much the same as the government's refugee settlement handbook. That's what you're starting to talk about tonight, figuring out how to get our family well established."

Judi wanted absolute clarity. "So the settlement plan is really just for us? It's nothing that has to be filed?"

"No, there's no more filing of anything. But there is one more critical piece of paper you need to know about. Only when all the screening, such as medical and security, is finished in Lebanon and Syria will our family will be approved to travel to Canada. When the transportation notice arrives, it's definitely full speed ahead for us. If, on the other hand, there's a problem and their application is denied, then our sponsorship will go to someone else. We'd get another family."

"You mean our family isn't for sure?"

"No. We'd get somebody else, though. All Saints probably gets two calls a week about refugees and people dropping off their family stories for me to read. It's sad; there's a lot. I'm trying to farm them out to other congregations, but there may not be enough of them. CLWR has a good allotment from the government of twenty-five refugees a month—individuals, not families—for private sponsorship." She reached for some grapes. "These are really ripe and good," she whispered as she took a second cluster.

Several people were uneasy about timelines, partly because of stories they'd heard of long waits followed by frantic activity. Sometimes people handle such anxiety with a flurry of comments and questions, and sometimes it is easier to deny and avoid. Tonight, they chose the latter approach and the conversation withered.

Would tonight's reluctance to take on leadership roles characterize the coming months? Time would tell, but already subtle group dynamics were emerging.

Vicki broke the lull. "This is a bit off topic, but it's bothering me. I saw a newspaper article last week about a sponsoring group in Ontario that was asked to switch the family they would be helping to one that was ready to come immediately. This raised an ethical dilemma about dumping their original family, with whom they'd already Skyped and built relationships. I wonder how likely it is that we might be asked to do the same."

Ellen bent forward in her chair. "I've heard of that case and think the chance of it happening to us is low. They were government-sponsored families versus a private sponsorship like ours, under a partnership between the government and their church allotment."

The partnership of the church and government didn't make sense to Vicki, but she chose not to pursue it. Her underlying concern was simply that delays meant more opportunity for things to go wrong. "So explain to me again why we can't yet meet with the sister in Surrey. Is it because of something here or in the Middle East?"

"The paperwork here apparently isn't finished. Noor said that should come very soon, and then I think the work shifts mainly to the overseas bureaucracy. At that point, he'd like to set up a meeting with the sister and a few from All Saints. In principle, all the welcoming team could go, but we don't want to overwhelm the sister. We would talk with her and find out how she wants to be involved."

Having a meeting with no chair could be frustrating. Shayla tried to get the group to address her workload concern. "It might be good to do a mind map and identify core areas, each with one of us as a lead person. The lead organizes a subgroup, and they all do the work. Maybe we can figure out tonight what those areas are. We all have different competencies and interests."

"Who likes to shop?"

"What kind of shopping?"

"The manual says 'learn to shop, newcomers' needs, national foods, Canadian foods, bargaining, cheap prices, economical discount stores.'"

"We might be getting ahead of ourselves. If it turns out the sister and her church community are involved, they might do that kind of stuff."

"Finances, interpreters, settlement services, transportation. What will be their language?"

"Arabic."

Pastor Ellen joined the free-for-all, picking up on language. "Remember that, at first, we need a translator who is not connected with them—one who is neutral. This may sound ridiculous, but we need to be certain that the translation is accurate, not a spin on what they'd like the person to hear. We don't yet know the dynamic between the sister and the incoming family. Once we're comfortable, we won't need an extra Arabic speaker."

She moved back to the topic of forming subgroups. "Maybe hold another kitchen table meeting after a Sunday service because going to a home can be a barrier for some people," she suggested. "I'm not saying to stop meeting in homes among your leadership group. It's just that, if you're wanting to reach out and involve others, meetings at coffee time after church will likely result in more people participating. It's convenient for them and less intimidating than going to the home of somebody they might not know very well, and where it's hard to withdraw graciously if things are different than what appeals to them."

"Let's keep in mind that Seattle can help," Judi said. "They could gather supplies like sheets. There might be somebody who's a cook who could come and be part of a kitchen weekend, or take our family around to learn to shop in Canada. You know, things like getting outfitted with school supplies."

The conversation meandered to a proposal to maintain a blog. "I like the idea of keeping a record of our journey," Vicki said. "Could we password protect our website, rather than have something that's totally public? Sometimes you write more freely and honestly when you know the whole world isn't able to read your stuff. Then we could edit it and decide what we want to say publicly."

Shayla supported the idea of a password but for a different reason. "I'm super aware of confidentiality. Before our family is here and safely settled, I wouldn't want to put anything online that could jeopardize their arrival."

The conversation lurched to a new topic. "Regarding our Seattle visit at the end of October," Judi said, "we need to respond to SRAG about the invitation. Nobody spoke to me after I announced it on Sunday, nor about joining this meeting tonight. Maybe we need to be specific and ask individuals directly."

Ellen presented a different perspective. "Not to discourage you going to Seattle, but it would be good to have them come up here first for another visit. I'll name my manipulative motive: the more at ease they feel in Vancouver, especially with homestays, the more certain we'll be of their help at crunch time. Incidentally, there may be others at All Saints who would be willing to accommodate our American friends in the future, having heard about the good experiences last month. Some people feel a little…I'm trying to find the right word. Not jealous. Just that they missed out."

Penny doubted the wisdom of switching the direction of the next visit. "I suspect they need some of us to go to Seattle so their broader community feels involved and gets a sense of who we are."

"Oh. The broader community reminds me that another church down there, Benediction Lutheran, has now joined and chipped in $5,000," Ellen said.

"Wow. Things, good things, just keep happening."

"They proposed three options and asked for All Saints' opinion," Ellen continued. "I said we might not express a strong preference because it's their funding. One option is just to dump the money into the kitty to provide more for our family each month. Another is to set it aside for startup costs. A third option is to start a fund for another refugee later, perhaps an LGBTQ person."

"And they'd just send an email to the Middle East to identify such a person?" Vicki asked skeptically.

"It's kind of an underground that gets people out so they can have a life with a partner," Ellen replied. "It could be complicated and would require a great deal of discretion, but it does happen."

Judi gave her preference. "I like keeping it for startup costs. That would give us a bit of a safety net. We could try to avoid drawing on it, with the idea that whatever's left at the end of, say, eighteen months would go towards the third option of another refugee sponsorship."

"I have a niggling worry," Shayla said. "Because the Badawi and Qatab families were at the meeting during the August visit from Seattle, they've heard about this enormous sum of money the Americans have raised. And now there's more. Are they in any way speculating there might be a little left over for them?" A few eyes widened at this remark, a valid concern.

"No," Pastor Ellen said. "These people are astonishing. There is no jealousy or expectation, even though they probably wouldn't complain about sharing any surplus. But do they have any expectations? No, none whatsoever.

"I know that if I was Partha, sitting there injured and experiencing how hard things are, and I heard about money for a family that's not even here yet, I might wonder if a few morsels could be thrown my way. He doesn't think that way. I might, but he doesn't. They're just grateful to be here. They'll struggle and scrape, but they'll make it. Partly with some help from relatives because families in that culture help each other. That's a good thing."

Ellen looked at her watch and bolted up. "I'm travelling tomorrow, so my alarm will go off at 5:00 a.m. I should have left ages ago. You've covered a lot of ground tonight. You're making progress, albeit circuitously. So long, everyone. Thanks, Vicki. I can let myself out." And then she made her way down the stairs.

Vicki signalled a small break. "The bathroom is the second door on the left, if anybody needs it. The kitchen is on the right if you want refills. Just help yourself anytime." Everyone stayed in the living room, and so the meeting resumed, returning to some topics that had been left dangling.

"I'd like to get information about agencies like ISS and MOSAIC," Judi said. "And also to speak to the Badawis, who know all the language training stuff. We need lists of doctors, stores, and other resources. What's with Welcome House that ISS runs?"

Penny pulled out her cell phone. "I'm quickly reading through the ISS website. I can't tell what's restricted to government-sponsored refugees. Maybe only certain services are restricted?"

Shayla responded, "Everyone is entitled to use ISS services, but Welcome House is where government-sponsored refugees stay for their first two weeks in Canada. Then they're basically on their own. That's what happened with the Iranian refugees we all met a few years ago. They had nobody to support them after the first two weeks."

"Wow," Judi gulped. "That is so scary. That's not good."

Shayla suggested, "How about us doing a bit of research about these agencies before we meet again?"

"Yes," Paul said with conviction. "We don't need to reinvent the wheel. We need to work smart rather than hard."

"In that vein, I need to read the sponsorship handbook more closely and develop a good grasp of it," Penny said. "I've seen it online, but I'm kind of a paper person. I'll get the church office to print a copy of the relevant chapters for each of us so we can sit around a table and go through them together."

The group adjourned with a promise to come to the next meeting, having done lots of homework about the services available in the community.

LEARNING ABOUT REFUGEES

The Refugees' Plight

To apply to enter Canada, refugees must complete a Canadian government form, *IMM0008: Schedule 2 – Refugees Outside Canada*, while overseas. A confidential document, it includes such personal information as the dates of birth of applicants and the full names of relatives. In addition to the standard release of this information to Canadian settlement service agencies and provincial health authorities, the father of our family, Yamo, authorized disclosure to the sponsoring group at All Saints. The following excerpts from Yamo's filing of Schedule 2 consist only of non-identifiable information about how his family came to flee their home in Syria and why they sought safety in a new land.

Do you and/or your family members understand English or French? If yes, explain where and when you and/or each of your family members learned it.

No. I received assistance in completing the application forms.

Have you ever been refused refugee status by the country in which you are currently living or by any other country?

No.

Have you ever applied for Convention refugee status with the United Nations High Commissioner for Refugees?

Yes. No result till now. No one called us since two years.

Set out in chronological order all the significant incidents that caused you to seek protection outside your home country.

In 2013, our house was invaded by ISIS. They obliged us to leave at night or will kill us. They obliged my wife to wear veil to leave. They stole all our possessions (jewels, money) so we just took our Bibles with us. They hit me and broke my knees without mercy and threw us out.

What protection, if any, did you seek from the authorities of your country?

Our country authorities are unable to protect us. As we all know the situation in Syria is so bad, the army is facing a very big difficulty in eliminating the terrorism. All Syrians run away and no one has hope to come back.

Describe the exact route of your journey to your present location.

We left our house, heading to our village by bus. We stayed around eight months before going to Lebanon in 2016 by bus. Then we took buses, heading to my sister-in-law place and we still there till present.

Will you be able to return to your home country?

No. How can we go back to Syria and we don't have any place there. ISIS became stronger and they are waiting for any Christians to kill him. I cannot take risk by losing my family. ISIS do not have pity for anybody and our country is unable to protect any one of us.

Are you free to work, attend school, and travel freely within the country where you currently live?

Lebanon is facing a very bad situation at all levels. They have a very critical economic crisis without neglecting the bad security situation. So we are unable to work in order to earn money and live with dignity.

Are you in danger in the country where you are now living?

Yes. We are facing a very bad security crisis in Lebanon, like all Lebanese. But we are facing an additional pressure because Lebanese fear Syrians because of ISIS, so we are not able to move freely in the country and live peacefully.

If applicable, provide additional information that will assist us in determining whether you meet the criteria for Canada's Refugee and Humanitarian Resettlement Program.

I am a father of children. We were driven out of places by ISIS. We lost all our possessions and money. We are jobless and hopeless. I need to ensure stability to my family. Lebanon is facing a very bad situation, and I do need to send them to school and raise them in a safe environment. We are Christians and will not accept to go back to Syria to join ISIS. We believe in God and believe that you can help us in order to be useful in the community. We are still young, full of energy and just need chance to start and improve ourselves.

Please help me to found a good family. I do not want anything for me. I just want to see my children happy and live their childhood like all kids. I need to be in a safe country well respected to live with dignity. I can do any job that allows us to live in peace.
Please help us.

The covering email from CLWR mentioned the name of the Orthodox church in the Vancouver area where Yamo's relative worshipped. It continued with some information about timelines.

"The papers CLWR prepared are already submitted to the centralized processing office. We should be getting the approval soon." However, the overseas process could take up to eight months after that approval.

October Chatter
The conversations at All Saints, some with members of the welcoming team, continued throughout the autumn and included a broad range of topics.

World Leader
– If this article in the *Vancouver Sun* is accurate, we may be helping our American friends become experts.
– What on earth are you talking about?
– Listen: October 11, 2016. Headline: US looks at emulating Canada's refugee plan—Private sponsors. The article begins: "The United States appears to be working towards a system for privately sponsoring refugees, potentially making it the latest country to emulate the program Canada has deployed during the Syrian crisis." I'll skip the next paragraphs. Then it says, "nearly half the Syrian refugees Canada brought in starting late last year entered through private or quasi-private initiatives."
– That's nice, but what's the big deal?
– Apparently Canada is a world leader in this, which is cool given that Canada is so often in the middle of the pack of Western nations regarding social and economic programs.
– Seriously?
– Yes. Listen to how the article ends. "'At least thirteen countries have made enquiries about emulating the program,' Immigration Minister John McCallum said. Australia and New Zealand have adopted such programs, and McCallum said the United Kingdom is working on one. He said he's happy to offer technical advice. 'We're

definitely the pioneers in this,' he said. 'I think this is a model that would be of some value all over the world.'"

– Who knew? I mean, I'm very aware that I'm unclear on the different types of refugee sponsorships in Canada—government, private, quasi-private—but I thought that was just me being confused. I had no idea we're involved in something progressive by world standards.

– Me too. But regardless, SRAG is getting a close-up look at how a private sponsorship program can operate. The American government won't necessarily adopt the same model as Canada, but at least SRAG will have some background to contribute to the conversation. That would be a great unexpected benefit from this project.

– Yes. And I've learned that a perceived expert isn't necessarily a person who knows a lot about a topic. Sometimes it's just whoever knows a smidgen more than anybody else in the room.

Cinema

– I know we've been anxious in case our family arrives on short notice, but let's think about the opposite problem.

– What's that? Going to the airport to find they weren't on the plane?

– No, taking months and months to come. It's already been a year since Karl and William got the ball rolling in Seattle, and it will probably be at least another half year before the family gets here. A year and a half, and that's a good-case scenario. What if it stretches out to two or more years? Some enthusiastic helpers may lose momentum and drift off. It could be deflating.

– I see what you mean.

– How can we keep people engaged when nothing is happening? It's the same problem the military faces in peacetime, and I think the answer is much the same.

– Namely?

– Education. Keep them learning.

– I'm not following you.

– Listen to a roundabout explanation. I once heard the difference between applied and pure research described as this: the goal of applied research is to build a better mousetrap, whereas pure research wants to learn things about mice that make mousetraps obsolete. That's the only long-run solution for refugees.

– You've lost me again.

– It doesn't matter how many refugees we take in and how well we help them, it's still only a drop in the bucket compared to all the displaced people in the world. Our taking in Syrian refugees is just building a better mousetrap. We need mousetraps right now, so what we're doing is good and essential. In the long run, though, we have to do our bit towards changing the world so there won't be any refugees fleeing their homeland, making refugee mousetraps obsolete, so to speak.

– Fair enough, but that's a tall order.

– Granted, but we can make a start. We already have a couple of dozen people in Seattle and Vancouver who are starting to see the world a little differently because of their involvement with this project. We have to keep promoting that. If all we do is aid five Syrians and leave unchanged a hundred or more Canadians and Americans who will eventually help in some way, we'll have missed a huge opportunity to take a tiny step towards building the kind of world where the notion of a refugee is an outdated concept.

– Like I said, fair enough, but how?

– That's where education comes in. When we're not busy running around getting ready for our family, it's a perfect time to get people reflecting on what they're seeing and hearing. Asking questions. Learning about parts of the world they had previously ignored. We need to find low-key, simple, enjoyable things that will help people broaden their horizons. That's all. Enjoyable horizon broadening.

– And you perhaps have some ideas on how to do this?

– Sort of. Here's an example. I happened to borrow a DVD from the library, *Amreeka,* about a Palestinian Christian family who goes to

Illinois. It didn't win any academy awards, but it's a decent little film. I think it would be a pleasant discussion starter in our congregations.
– In what way?
– It starts in Palestine, in the West Bank. The scenery and buildings probably aren't all that different from Syria. More importantly, it shows ordinary people doing ordinary things in a tough situation. It makes them seem real, not stereotypes. The family is just as dysfunctional as most of ours. The teenage boy gets mouthy at a checkpoint on the way home from school in Israel, which helps the mother decide that they have to leave that toxic situation. They manage to make it to America where the film's themes include homesickness, trying to fit in, shame at underemployment, and prejudice—all things our family is likely to encounter.
– Not to mention that some in our congregations already have experienced these. It would be great if we could tease out their stories.
– Exactly. These are the first tiny steps through which God brings about change in society.
– There must be plenty of other international films that would be good discussion starters.
– I expect so. I just know that this one is in our local library. It may also be available through iTunes or Netflix. There's even an article about it in Wikipedia. I found it interesting how the filmmaker modelled the family and a high school principal on her own life.

Language Learning

"I work at a textiles place," Penny said. "Using sewing machines is visual, not oral, so we can hire people with weak language skills. At the moment, we have two Syrian fellows who are full-time employees and a Syrian woman who is doing an unpaid stint to gain experience. Our two Syrians are excellent employees and they learn super quick. They're happy to be working and contributing.

"We're apparently very successful at employing former refugees and this seems to have brought our firm on to every agency's radar. For example, a woman from MOSAIC phoned because she heard of us from the BC Manufacturers Association. WorkBC also knows about us. As a result, help is coming out of the woodwork, and I've learned quite a bit about supports for refugees in the past three months.

"The MOSAIC woman said the federal government now has a grant competition for innovative programs for learning English while working. Language is so important, and the thinking used to be that newcomers shouldn't work during the first year so that they could attend ESL classes. The rationale was that, if somebody's working full time and commuting to and from work, the last thing they want to do when they get home is go to English classes at night. The tide seems to be turning, though, with the thinking now that some work might be desirable.

"MOSAIC is trying to get funding for a language app since everybody seems to have cell phones. If a worker has a fifteen-minute break, they can pull up the app and do a little studying. The language content is all workplace oriented. MOSAIC asked if we'd be involved in a pilot project. We immediately said, 'Sure!' No matter what happens, the app will be of benefit to our employees.

"Our Syrians are doing quite well with language learning because there's only two of them. Because we have so many languages in our workforce, English has to be the common or base language. Some factories are all Chinese or all South Asian, so those workers keep talking in their original language. We however are so diverse that we don't have second language cliques. In fact, we have a deaf woman who I once saw communicating in an improvised sign language at the bus stop with one of our other employees. It was very cute.

"I'm learning there are a lot of support organizations, and many new things are being tried. It's quite exciting, actually. Our operations manager can make a phone call and get a translator on the line. This is great when she's trying to give safety information or complicated instructions; she just phones and gets her instructions translated. She says it's a phenomenal service and it's free. And there are tools like Google Translate—not perfect, by any means, but they help.

"In any event, I'm not necessarily of the mindset that newcomers have to be in language school for a year. For men especially, it may be important to get working."

Paul joined in. "At the college where I used to work, all the English as a Second Language classes, and they were pretty high level, used to be offered to ESL students before they moved into regular academic programs. Eventually, the college tried to provide some overlap so that a student could take, say, a biology course at the same time as an ESL class where the instructor had a science background and would tailor the vocabulary towards science. This is similar to what might happen in the workplace, learning English vocabulary that's relevant rather than generic, learning about how to order, say, lobster at a racetrack in New York."

"Learning while working is more practical for the person," Judi said. "You use the new learning, whereas in the classroom you go home without practicing and speak your native language. At least, that was my experience in my long process of learning English."

Vicki pondered this challenge to conventional wisdom. "There's probably a happy medium between learning on the job and in the classroom. I think you pretty much have to start in the classroom. It probably also depends on the learner."

Shayla shared her story. "When I came to Canada from Germany, I already spoke high school English, but I felt like my brain capacity was shrinking. To talk and think in another language with insufficient vocabulary and broken syntax is an exhausting cognitive load. You feel like you're dumb.

"Many newcomers have been away from school for a long time or never had much schooling. To sit in a classroom could be excruciating. This is why language classes sometimes simulate real life with, say, a cooking session with area-specific vocabulary."

Penny's personal experience was from a different perspective. "My first husband was German. At my in-laws', the family would speak in German, and I didn't know what they were saying. I'd hear my name every once in a while, and I'd think they were talking about me. It would make me quite angry.

"Once I was in their house, having now picked up enough German to get the gist of what they were saying, and I answered in English. They were taken back. After that, all the conversation was in English. It's very alienating when you don't know the language."

Sponsorship Workshop
– I went to a sponsorship workshop ten days ago offered by a group whose purpose seems to be to encourage all the different agencies and individuals to work together. It wasn't specific and I didn't find it as helpful as I'd hoped. They spent too much time telling us what we already know about the refugee crisis. One of the speakers was supposed to talk about sponsoring a family, but he could hardly speak English and just said how nice it was. I expected a Syrian newcomer to talk about her experiences and needs, but she was shy and just said how thankful she was.

I already knew many things. Sponsors are supposed to assist, not do everything for newcomers. Don't set them up with a good lifestyle and high expectations because if they don't get a job after the year is up, they'll be on welfare. They're typically really happy in the first year just to be here. Once they're here, don't call them refugees.

My breakout group included two young Syrian women brought over by their sister, who was busy with her own young family. One looked the same age as my kids, so I asked how old she was, to the mild horror of some in my group. She was twenty-seven and said she rather wished someone other than her sister had sponsored her because her sister didn't have time to show her anything. She said, "I hear there's lots of Syrians in Canada. I don't know how to meet them." She's gradually making contact, though, feeling less isolated.

This twenty-seven year old spoke English well, was university educated. The other woman didn't speak a word of English and was very shy.

Travel Loan

– When our family arrives, they'll be saddled with a government loan for their flights to Canada and medical exams when overseas. Can we use any of the money collected for the first year of settlement towards paying off that loan?

– Even with all the money from the two churches in Seattle, our family is still going to be living in poverty. What's the priority? Should it be getting them through the month decently and trusting that they'll have jobs in a few years' time so they can make repayment? I wouldn't want to deprive them of groceries right now to pay off a loan that's due in the distant future.

– And yet, maybe we should make partial loan repayment a tiny item in the budget right from the get-go. It might be a learning opportunity for them that this country is not Santa Claus.

– I've heard different viewpoints about loan repayment. In one interview on CBC radio, people described being saddled with debt as truly horrific because they were unemployed. However, in extenuating circumstances, such as no job, you can apply for a deferral. Other newcomers said having to repay the loan instilled a sense of gratitude for all Canada had done for them. Repayment was a way of saying thank you. They didn't want to be charity cases.

– In a similar vein about not being dependent, a woman at the workshop I attended mentioned how the family she helped sponsor wanted more bicycles. One family member already had a bike and had found it enabled him to travel all over. She could easily have got them bikes, but instead she taught them how to use Craigslist. When she came back a week later, the family had found used bikes on the internet, bargained, and got themselves some cheap bikes and fixed them up. They were riding their bikes when she arrived, proud of themselves.

– Teaching them how to fish, not giving them fish.

Housing Location

Housing location had been broached before, but never resolved. Committee members came at the issue from different angles, some more flexible about location than others.

– The settlement handbook says we can stipulate that the family live in our proximity so we can actually support them. We have to set things up so we can meet our responsibilities. I'm not going to drive a long way over congested bridges.

– I'm willing to make those drives if it turns out that a bunch of distant people who know Syrian culture are able to provide good support. I'll go out of my way if it serves the family better.

– But then it will be different. We wouldn't have contact every day or two.

– Agreed, it could be very different.

– We'd have to liaise with another group of people.

– Yes. In that case, we might have more of an overseeing role, ensuring the family's needs are met by others rather than meeting them ourselves. Our responsibility is just to see that the jobs get done. Another consideration is that I don't want to temporarily settle our family in one community if it's clear they want to live somewhere else. I don't want to disrupt kids in school or help find new physicians.

– We can't rely on others. Remember how quickly Zrebar's sister packed up shop when her husband got a job overseas? The Badawis thought they had plenty of support from their relatives when they arrived, but that ended. All Saints then became their go-to.

– True enough. That's why I still have an open mind about location. When we find out about the sister and church, we might not especially like them. I doubt that will be the case, but we might not want to work closely with them. I want more information before we decide where we want to go searching for housing.

– Here's another consideration. I'm not for a moment suggesting that we do something similar, but a woman in my hiking group last Monday told me how her Unitarian church chose a location for their refugee family back in January. They wanted housing close to a particular school in Southeast Burnaby.

– Why for Pete's sake would they do that? BC schools are fairly consistent in quality.

– Because the neighbourhood is low income and ethnically diverse, one school has been designated as a community school. This means that, in addition to the usual educational programs, a number of social services and workers are based there. The woman's daughter teaches at the school and knows how to navigate the system to access support. So this is obviously a special case, but it goes to show that we need to think expansively when deciding about house location and not just latch on to the first suitable idea that comes to mind.

Oh, and the other thing she told me is quite scary. Last autumn, they budgeted $700 per month for a two-bedroom apartment. That sounds awfully low to me, but it's a poor neighbourhood and maybe they were being realistic. Be that as it may, with all the nutty things that have been happening in the overheated Vancouver real estate market recently, vacancies plummeted and they ended up paying almost $1,200 for a one bedroom. Things changed that fast.

Identification

– I heard a suggestion that all of us on the committee should have a photo taken with our names and phone numbers so that, when our family needs to call us for something, they know who they're calling. Likewise, it helps when somebody comes to their home. This would be especially important in the first few weeks. We could turn the photos into fridge magnets and stick them on their fridge.

The photos would add another level of protection against scammers who might contact them. It also helps with just a lack of trust. Remember where they're coming from—where fear might kick in just from answering the door.

Canada Child Benefit Program
– If I'm correctly understanding what I heard, and assuming it's accurate information, our family could receive something like $15,000 annually for their children from the Canada Child Benefit Program. I had no idea the amounts were so large for families with a very low income.
– Wow. This is from the federal government?
– Yes. I think the program started just a few months ago, a promise in last spring's federal budget. Probably the new government wanting to make a splash while it eliminates other grants. It's for all citizens and permanent residents.
– Including refugees?
– I think so, but we need to confirm this. For kids under age six, the maximum is something like $6,500 a year. It drops by $1,000 for school age kids. Families with an income less than $30,000 annually get the maximum grant for each child. Families with a higher income get smaller grants.
– No wonder the settlement handbook said to apply for child benefits within a day or two of arrival. Even if the funding turns out to be only half the amount you mentioned, it's still significant.

Terrorism
– Perhaps everything worthwhile in life involves an element of risk.
– Come again?
– Well, moving away from home for a first job or college, getting married, joining a new group—you're taking a chance it won't work out.
– What got you thinking along these lines?

– Maybe it's due to the American presidential election and all Donald Trump is doing to stoke fears about immigration, but too often it feels like there's an unspoken fear of terrorism lurking in the background when I talk to others about Syrian refugees. Getting involved in the lives of other people, especially people we don't know, is risky.

– I know. Fear of terrorism, in contrast to a watchful prudence, is irrational when you look at the odds of encountering all the other types of violence in our society. Let's face it, though, humans are not especially rational.

– It's so discouraging when the fears come from people who claim they have faith in God and talk about grace freely given through Christ.

– Yes, sometimes it's inconsistent and irrational, but often it comes from a good place—a desire to protect the people and values we cherish—and not from a selfish desire to maintain privileged lives.

– I suppose. It's just that I feel powerless in trying to allay these fears.

– If it helps, I saw a piece that originated with the *Montreal Gazette* this month. It talked about some study of college students in Quebec that found the youths who were most supportive of violence were less likely to identify as religious than those who did not support violence. The study is shaking some popular assumptions about religion and radicalization.

– One study. Big deal.

– I admit it's far from conclusive, but doesn't this finding mesh with your personal experiences? What proportion of the violent people you've encountered had much of a faith? The study also found that second generation immigrants had a higher likelihood of radicalization than first-generation immigrants.

– Interesting. If that's true, then perhaps the risk of terrorism is not so much a problem with immigrants or religion but due to other factors. Social or economic exclusion, for example.

– Yes, maybe. I'm sure the causes of radicalization are complex, and the study just scratched the surface. Its value for me is that it makes us question the taken-for-granted assumptions about terrorism and radicalization, and that's a good thing. When people start questioning, seeking data, and having open discussion, they often reach healthy conclusions.

– Sometimes. Sometimes by the grace of God.

More and More Learning

The welcoming team was still settling into Vicki's living room for another short meeting when Shayla spoke. A navy blue binder rested in her lap, the three rings open to receive the thin document in her left hand. "Hey, did you see this in chapter seven of the handbook about having to sponsor other family members as well?"

"What are you talking about?"

"It's right here about newcomers having the right to sponsor other family members within a year. We're obligated to look after them as well."

"What!"

She tilted the page forward for better lighting. "It says, 'Your settlement planning should also take into account the settlement needs of non-accompanying family members listed"—she took a deep breath—"on the IMM0008, as your group will be expected to sponsor them as well if they submit an IMM0008 within one year of the arrival of the principal applicant.'"

The movement in the room stopped. "Does that mean aunts and uncles and grandparents, or just the five people we already know about who might arrive at different times?"

"I don't know. I'm not sure I understand this, but we'd better have a good look at that IMM form and see how many names are listed. If there are just five names, then perhaps we can forget about this issue. Otherwise, that's definitely something else for us to look into."

"I feel like I'm getting drawn into more than I intended," Vicki said. "That's not necessarily bad, but there's so much to learn. Always something more. I guess it's good we're starting early and that there's a group of us to do the sleuthing."

"Yeah, it takes a village, as the saying goes. That's why the Immigrant Services Society put out a call for volunteers to help orient newcomers. Everything from playgroups for kids, how to use transit, help with language and housing. Fortunately, over 5,000 people came forward to volunteer."

"The Badawis are some of those volunteers."

"To help newcomers with housing after they leave Welcome House," Judi continued, "the ISS apparently scoured developers and landlords for vacancies. That's how so many Syrians came to live in the Western Cedar apartment complex up the hill from us."

"I heard those were teardown buildings, but that ISS convinced the developer to hold off demolition and rent them in bulk to ISS for occupancy by refugees."

"Yes. And then, in making some minor electrical modifications to keep the building functional, something went wrong and that's how the fire started. Now the building sits empty until it's demolished. There's no point making big repairs after a fire to a building that's about to come down. What a tragedy for the occupants who have already been through so much."

The thought hung in silence as people digested what they'd heard. The formal meeting had not even begun. They'd anticipated learning a great deal, but it took time to process and absorb all the new information. Although it was energizing and broadening, it was also humbling and daunting.

"Going back to the manual," Vicki said, "it emphasizes that the first few days are critical. The first impression the family gets sets the tone for their first weeks and months in Canada. We have to give attention to both their practical and their emotional needs.

"For example, in the manual, there's some practical stuff about the first day that might not even occur to us. When they get into their housing, wherever and whatever it might be, we have to make sure they know how to turn on faucets, operate the telephone, and use the oven or microwave."

"Don't underestimate the importance of such basic stuff when you're changing cultures," Paul said. "When I was in Delhi, you should have seen me trying to figure out how to turn on the shower. There were about five knobs, two showerheads, and a faucet—a whole control panel—and this was a budget hotel. I never did find the hot water."

"I'm not so sure I'd want to see you buck naked in the shower," Judi said, "even if you were entertaining as you fiddled with things. But I did see that section in the manual you're talking about, Vicki. I recall it saying that, in the first few days, we need to help with applying for a social insurance number, medical coverage, and the child tax benefit."

"And also during the first couple of days," Vicki continued, "assuming they're not super jetlagged or sick, we need to take them on a tour of their neighbourhood, show them how and where to shop for food and clothing, and open a bank account.

"I'm seeing how information overload is going to be a problem at the beginning. Yet it's hard to avoid if we want to encourage them to make their own decisions and become independent right from the get-go."

Paul pulled out his copy of chapter seven. "The chart on page 83 about cultural adjustment is good. I love the names for the typical stages of adjustment: honeymoon, challenge and crisis, recovery, and cultural adjustment. And the explanations of each stage are really helpful. I had thought about initial confusion, loneliness and homesickness, but not about the possibility of depression or how stresses could play out differently by gender. If somebody's depressed, they might not have the energy to do the things they need to do. So things get worse and they dig themselves into a deeper pit."

"Yes," Shayla said. "It's easier for us just to plan for the practical needs and gloss over the emotional support we'll need to provide. The emotional stuff is hard."

"True enough," Penny said, "but care and compassion will go a long way towards compensating for any lack of skill or knowledge we might have on the emotional side. I believe it's love, not laughter, that is the best medicine."

The conversation seemed productive, but Shayla thought it was time for the formal meeting to start. The absence of a committee chair still had its downside in her view. "To continue from our last meeting about the various settlement agencies and services, our school district has a long history of dealing with refugees." Heads nodded in agreement. "They have settlement workers, English language training. They liaise with the mental health people and with the Ministry of Children and Family Development, and also with the regional health authority. They have welcome centres where they do assessments and help children settle into the schools."

"You mean they have separate programs before they throw children into mainstream classrooms?"

"Maybe just some services, not whole programs. I don't think it's all that separate, though. Kids pretty much get thrown into things right away. Hopefully, many of the schools have settlement workers."

"What my friend Wendy said made it sound like immigrants kids all go to one area when they get English assistance. She said the youngest ones get placed first into regular classrooms because they pick things up so quickly. Can you imagine what it would be like to be high school age, hardly speaking any English, and walk straight into a regular classroom? Older kids have to learn to interpret social cues, and they don't have an adult looking after them the way little kids do. I'm glad they might get a bit of preparation, however fleeting."

"I'll bet the school district is able to prepare them only minimally," Penny speculated. "Some of these kids come from a war zone and may never have attended school for more than a few months at a time. They may be nine or ten and have essentially no schooling. The school district here assesses them to determine which classes they need to be placed in. It's tough to balance academic background with social and cultural considerations.

"The school probably needs time to apply for funding so they can have English and other supports available when the refugees arrive in regular classrooms. Some sort of plan has to be put in place for the child."

"If kids go to a centre for orientation, I hope it does a variety of things with them, not just academics."

"Such as?"

"Perhaps like taking them on a field trip to the police station so they understand that police in Canada are safe people, not corrupt."

Paul felt this was an appropriate time to contribute his findings. "Let me tell you what I found on the web about a language training program. It's called Language Instruction for Newcomers to Canada. The acronym, LINC, is pronounced 'link.' The federal government funds it, so it's free for the participants. It serves adults, not kids, who I presume go through the school system."

Paul fumbled with his notes, flipping a page before finding what he was seeking. "It offers English from Level 1, low beginner, to high intermediate. There's also a pre-beginner literacy level for someone who doesn't have any English. Canadian citizens and visitors are not eligible for LINC, just newcomers to the country. The process is that they go and do a language placement test. Everybody who lives in our part of Greater Vancouver goes to a centre in Surrey for the assessment. You complete a form on the internet and then contact the assessment office to get an appointment."

Penny asked, "Do you mean they do an initial assessment on the net?"

"No, but I don't know what the form is for. Someone will have to take the refugees over to Central Surrey and wait for them to complete their testing. After the assessment, that office provides a list of all the places in the region that offer the recommended course level. The refugees can choose, probably based on transportation more than anything, which school they want to go to. Sometimes there are waiting lists, so that's a problem. They can only be on one school's waiting list at a time. A referral counsellor can help them choose.

"Classes could be in the morning, afternoon, or evening. Full-time classes are usually twenty-five hours a week. Part-time classes are between nine and fifteen hours a week. Most classes seem to be Monday to Friday, but there seem to be weekend options too. Some of the schools have free childcare for preschoolers."

"Get out!" Vicki shouted. Paul stiffened. "Sorry, Paul," she said. "The cat knows she's not allowed in here. She normally stays downstairs. I don't know what's got into her tonight."

"I'm glad I didn't have my mug in my hand, or you would have been cleaning coffee off your ceiling." He settled back into the armchair and continued. "Most classes start at the beginning of the month. Overall, my impression is that there's a very established process that works smoothly."

"Is that the only option? Are there other ways for adults to get language training?"

"I think that's the only one that's free because it's government funded. There are scads of little language schools in BC where students pay tuition. For all I know, some of these schools might be contracted by the government to offer LINC classes. And various agencies probably have little conversation clubs for a few hours each week."

"When I came to Canada," Judi said, "I studied in this type of class. It didn't matter where you came from, as long as you were a newcomer. You had a year or two to study and learn English. Many of my classmates were refugees, whereas I was a regular immigrant. This was free, but I didn't know about it when I first came to Canada. I went to a private school initially got charged $500 or $600 per course, and those prices were decades ago. The private schools were so expensive."

"Language is crucial. Newcomers can be very aware of their language levels. It's an essential stepping stone."

"The levels are standardized across Canada. I expect every ESL teacher would be familiar with the assessment test. Each skill— reading, writing, listening, and speaking—is tested. You might be different levels on different skills. Actually, you probably will. I don't know whether there are separate classes for each of these skills or whether students get placed in a level that's an average of all their skills."

"Have I mentioned I'm so impressed you typed up these notes?" Penny clasped her hands to heart and tilted her head upwards. "What dedication and class." Vicki quietly guffawed.

Paul ignored the two women. "Language assessment is something we'll need to start working on during the first week. There will be housing, telephone, banking, and those sorts of things to deal with, but because of the potential waiting lists and classes that start just once a month, we'll need to get moving on language.

"Language is one big issue that I'm now feeling calmer about," he said, "knowing how the system works and that it's well established. The more we can learn about other things, like getting started with health care, the better. Housing, on the other hand, is still a big concern for me. There's no system, just the law of the jungle, with high rents, low vacancies, and wait lists for non-market housing."

"Shouldn't we prepare a rough budget that we can give to the family to get them started?" Judi asked. "We also need some accountability so that, for example, they don't take portions of the money and send it back to family in Syria. And do it in a way that's not stepping on the family's toes."

"Cell phones can be a lifeline, especially if you're lost and don't speak the language. We should give our family an idea of what would be an appropriate plan and the cost."

"Cell phones in Canada are super expensive compared to much of the world," Penny observed. "Over there, they probably just go to a corner store and get a prepaid phone."

"I don't have data on my plan. Everywhere I go, work and home, has WiFi."

"We can't assume our family will live somewhere with internet immediately. It may make sense to have one really good plan for one person in the family so they can always get information off the internet at anytime. Bus schedules and Google maps, for example."

"What about getting a car?"

"I don't think we have the money. Bus passes."

"Four or five bus passes aren't cheap either. I wonder if there are any subsidies for low income people."

"They might not even have a driver's licence, at least not one they can use in Canada."

"Access to public transit will be another constraint on housing choice."

Shayla had long finished adding papers to her binder and was now flipping through it. "Another part of the budget is the immigration loan repayment. That's about the cost of their medical screening overseas and their flight."

"Is the government still doing that? I thought repayment had been cancelled, at least for the 25,000 refugees."

"I don't know. The manual just says 'The first written demand for repayment will be mailed shortly after the newcomers arrive.' The loan is interest-free for a certain period of time, and they have something like five years to pay it off. There are possibilities for deferrals. That would be a good question to ask one of the agencies."

"We'll need somebody to do accounting about what money has flowed in and what has been paid out. Keeping track will be a crucial piece."

"It doesn't have to be double entry bookkeeping to the exact dollar, but we do need a general idea of financial flows, even if we're not the ones touching the money."

"Including if we do any top-up fundraising."

"I could keep track of money," Vicki volunteered. "That's my occupation, monitoring money. Setting the budget, though, is somebody else's decision."

"Speaking of fundraising," Paul said, "we need to know about the source of the Seattle funds. If it's all from individuals in a congregation, that's one thing. If there are organizations making donations, then we don't want to get caught in an embarrassing situation like some local environmentalists encountered when they were accused of being fronts for international organizations."

Penny agreed. "Yes, people are all fussed about funding sources right now. With all the talk about Vancouver's inflated housing market and money laundering through real estate and casinos, we need to be fully informed. I'm not suggesting anything bad will happen, just that everything needs to be transparent."

The conversation turned to an initial polling of who still wanted to visit Mount Olivet and who else might now be able to come. As the supply of cheese and crackers was rapidly declining, the meeting soon concluded.

Networks

The number of service providers in the wider community who support refugees and newcomers to Canada initially overwhelmed the welcoming team. "I vaguely knew such organizations existed," one member said, "but I really hadn't paid attention to what they do or how many there are. Now I'm keenly interested." Determining which would be helpful and which would be a distraction became a task of its own.

With over forty percent of Metro Vancouver's 2.5 million people born outside of Canada, the effective integration of immigrants into the social and economic life of the community was in everyone's best interest. Social support systems to foster the success of newcomers have increasingly replaced the sink-or-swim mentality of past generations, the rationale being that prevention is both cheaper and more humane than attempts at remediation. Some of these supports are available through MOSAIC, one of the largest settlement organizations in Canada, which has a $20 million annual budget, 300 staff, 450 regular volunteers and 300 contractors.

MOSAIC, short for Multi-Lingual Orientation Service Association for Immigrant Communities, describes itself as a registered charity serving immigrant, newcomer, and refugee communities in Greater Vancouver for the past forty years. It also explicitly mentions services for the LGBTQ and temporary foreign worker communities. These services, provided at thirty-two sites, include settlement assistance, English language training, employment programs, interpretation and translation, and counselling.

All Saints was on the MOSAIC mailing list, and every once in a while, the church office forwarded an email to the welcoming team. This message of October 20, 2016, was a typical email:

Subject: Update Refugee Related Events and Programs in Metro Vancouver Area

Dear Faith and Wider Refugee Support Community,

Once again, please find attached several events that are happening in the Metro Vancouver Area with regard to refugee issues. Please share this with anyone you may think would be interested.

Metro Vancouver Refugee Response Team **Networking Event about Private Sponsorship** on November 5 in North Vancouver (details attached). This event will provide information on cultural sensitivity in working with refugees, give opportunities to learn and discuss settlement issues and approaches, stories from refugees, and networking with private sponsors and other volunteers.

MOSAIC together with WorkBC is running a **"Hope to Work"** research project in November 2016 and February 2017. Details are attached. This is a great opportunity for many of the people you may be assisting. More details available upon request.

Engaging Dialogue Series, Challenges to Building Community within Canadian Diversity, on October 30, 2016, at Shaughnessy Heights United Church in Vancouver (details attached).

University of British Columbia REFUGEE SYMPOSIUM & OPERA—Breaking the Cycle: Canada's Refugee Record on the Global Stage. A multi-day symposium at UBC, alongside an opera and an art exhibit titled *The Consul* in order to stimulate discussion on the various aspects of the global refugee crisis. Operatic performances will take place on campus and at community venues—adjoined by conversation featuring prominent academics, community leaders, people who came to Canada as refugees, and impassioned advocates.

The networking event was organized by the Metro Vancouver Refugee Response Team, an organization whose vision was "to ensure that all refugees in Metro Vancouver have access to the information, services, and supports to ease their settlement and expedite their integration into the community." The agenda for the three-hour session at a city library was extensive:

- Overview of the Metro Vancouver Refugee Response Team

- Overview of the private sponsorship program
- Cultural sensitivity in working with refugees
- Working with refugees who might have experienced loss or grief
- What does it mean to be sponsored by a private group? Reflections from a recently arrived newcomer
- Settlement issues and approaches—best practices in working with refugees
- Small group discussions and networking

The Hope To Work (H2W) Program was advertised as a research project; however, "pilot project funded by the federal and provincial governments" might have been a better descriptor. It was a two-week program for thirty individuals, who would receive a training allowance for participation. A comparison group of thirty other individuals would receive an honorarium for completing surveys for the research team. The program included career planning, job search, and tours of four workplaces to help illustrate hiring needs. Participants had to be unemployed refugees who had lived in Canada for fewer than ten years, have at least a Grade 10 education or equivalent, and be fluent in Arabic or spoken English at Canadian Language Benchmark level 4 or higher.

MORE ACTIVE
ENGAGEMENT

The Sister Who Wasn't

Joanna, council chair at All Saints, sent a note to say that Immigration Canada had received the CLWR submission for All Saints' refugee family. Noor, in the local office of CLWR, now wanted to facilitate a meeting with the sister, one that was eventually set for October 24 at 5:00 p.m. The sister spoke English, so no interpreter would be needed. In conveying this information, Paul cautioned against becoming too excited.

"My understanding of the immigration approval is just that the application paperwork from CLWR has been completed to the government's satisfaction. The family will now be interviewed and a background check conducted in Lebanon, along with the medical examinations. It could be a long time before the family flies to Canada."

"Unfortunately, I'm only available during school hours," Shayla lamented, "as I have driving duties for the kids after school. I hate to not be at this meeting!"

Paul shared Shayla's disappointment that she wouldn't be present. He proposed that he take on taxi duty instead, if her kids felt comfortable with him, so she could attend. "I think you're better at this type of meeting than I am, plus the sister may be a bit more open if she's talking to other women. If this isn't a good option, you don't need to be tactful in saying so." He expressed his surprise at the late hour of the meeting, speculating it might have something to do with the sister's availability.

Shayla appreciated the offer, but she also had to be in North Vancouver that evening for a workshop. "There's no way I can make this meeting time. Aaargh…you remember those years?"

Ten days later, Vicki glanced at her watch as she stepped out of her grey Mazda. *Five to five, just in time*, she thought. Glancing up, she saw Paul pull into the church parking lot.

An unfamiliar sedan sat in the corner of the lot, near the 1950s bungalow that now housed the offices of the British Columbia Synod of the Evangelical Lutheran Church in Canada. A cigarette dangled from the driver's mouth. It was hard to see if the passenger was a woman. Paul wondered if this might be the sister of the Mousa family. Vicki and Paul lingered between their cars while Vicki searched unsuccessfully in her purse for a pen. The couple in the other car gave no sign of leaving their vehicle. Vicki and Paul ambled through the bungalow's empty carport to the back entrance.

A potted Japanese maple teetered at the top of three concrete steps leading down into the basement. No sign indicated whether this was the entrance to the Western office of the Canadian Lutheran World Relief, but the white door rested slightly ajar. Paul shrugged at Vicki and entered carefully. Peering into an office to the right, he saw a man in a knitted cap at a desk. "Noor," Paul guessed. "I'm Paul from All Saints."

Noor rose as Paul stepped aside to let Vicki introduce herself.

"We're just across the hall," Noor said, directing them.

The room's décor was early non-profit—no corporate glitz here to push up administrative overhead—with tables, chairs, a photocopier and other office paraphernalia. A short woman squinted at Paul as she stood to greet them. "You must be Oreva," Paul said. "We spoke on the phone a week or so ago to arrange this meeting. I'm Paul."

Oreva nodded and beckoned them to a table around the corner where two middle-aged women in western clothes sat. "Please have a seat and then I will make introductions."

Paul took the farthest chair and pushed aside telephone lines that stretched from the wall to a speaker phone at the end of the table. Vicki sat beside him, directly in front of a box of Middle Eastern sweet pastry nibbles. *Looks like a large box of chocolates I'd bring as a hostess gift*, she thought. Noor brought large white mugs of tea for everyone.

Natalie was the more outgoing of the two women. A Syrian who had come to Canada two decades ago and one of the first refugees to arrive, she spoke English fluently. She explained that she lived in Surrey, close to the American border, and owned a small driving school. Rona was Iraqi, also a Christian, but she had been in Canada for only a year and a half. Slowly it dawned on Paul that Rona's command of English was minimal.

"We're so pleased to meet all of you," Vicki said, looking first at the women and then turning to the staffers who had taken seats a few feet from the end of the table. "Now, just to help me keep everybody straight, I understand, Natalie, that you are either the sister or sister-in-law of Yamo or his wife, Leandra?"

"You are asking about the Mousas' relatives?" Natalie asked. "I do not know them." At this unexpected response, Vicki leaned forward and Paul straightened. "But this lady, Rona, lived beside the Mousa family in Lebanon. She was also a refugee there."

Paul glanced at Noor, whose deadpan expression gave no indication of whether he too had received incorrect information regarding relatives. Seeing the perplexed expression on Paul's face, Natalie continued. "I wanted to bring my brother to Canada, but he wouldn't leave Syria because our elderly father in Damascus is dying. I had already made contact with Noor and Oreva at CLWR, and we enjoyed working with each other. Then when I heard the

Mousas' story from Rona at my driving school, I thought I had to help them instead. I switched overnight."

Footsteps sounded in the hallway and Penny entered the room. Paul introduced her, explaining she had come straight from work. "I would have been here earlier," Penny said, "except I stood upstairs ringing the front doorbell. Only after waiting and waiting did I pull out my smartphone and re-read the email. Oops, downstairs, not upstairs. Everyone upstairs had gone home already."

Noor reached for a pastry, but they were packed so tightly he was unable to grip one. He lifted the plastic tray from the box, bent the edge back, and pried out a nut-filled baklava. After a polite pause, Penny followed suit.

Vicki pulled a sheet of paper from her clipboard and handed it to Natalie. "Here is the name and phone number of our church. The picture is of our pastor, our priest."

Natalie examined the sheet. "You have a woman priest?"

"Yes. The five names at the bottom are the welcoming committee who will be helping the Mousa family. One lady who is not here today comes from Germany and the other is from Hong Kong. We three were born in Canada, but these others know what it's like to come to a new country and have to learn English."

"I think I might know where this church is," Natalie said. This seemed to indicate she had come to this meeting not knowing exactly who was sponsoring the Mousa family. "It is near the hospital, yes?"

"That's right."

Oreva stepped to the table. "Before you put the paper away, could I make a photocopy for the file?" Taking the sheet, she quickly made a copy and returned the original to Natalie.

"These are just some of the people who will be helping," Penny said. "Plus there are the people in Seattle."

Natalie looked at her quizzically. Once again, she seemed to be taken off guard.

"There are some Americans who want to help Syrians, but it can be very difficult for Syrian refugees to enter America." Natalie nodded in agreement, apparently well familiar with the situation. "This church in Seattle, another Lutheran church, contacted CLWR to see if they could help Canadians bring more Syrian refugees into Canada. They partnered with us and are sending money so that we can help the Mousa family. We didn't have the money to do it ourselves, so we are most grateful for their help and caring."

Natalie's eyes widened. "Oh, God is so marvellous," she said with a broad smile. Vicki wondered why Natalie did not communicate this news to Rona but said nothing. Perhaps she would do so after the meeting had ended.

"Yes," Penny agreed. "God has brought many of us together to help this family." She extended an open hand. "You two, and CLWR, and us at All Saints church, and our friends in Seattle. All of us are doing a little to help out."

Incomplete and incorrect communication seemed to be forming the backdrop for the meeting, a challenge that was not unexpected but disappointing nonetheless. The upside was that everyone in the room seemed sensible, friendly, and committed. *We'll just have to work our way through any problems and misunderstandings*, thought Vicki. *We can do this.*

Preliminaries completed, the All Saints people looked to Noor for leadership. He chose not to provide any. *Might explain their choice of seating*, thought Paul. *I wonder if they are assessing how competent All Saints laypeople might be in organization and intercultural communication. Maybe that's why Noor asked, when we arrived, if Pastor Ellen would be attending.*

Paul felt he should step in, although he lacked an agenda for the meeting, because nobody else was speaking. "Perhaps you could tell us about the Mousa family? We're of course very eager to learn about them."

"Didn't you get the government paper?" Natalie asked.

"Yes, we just know the little that appeared on the form. It's really just a few sentences."

Natalie turned to Rona, which suggested that Natalie was less knowledgeable than the All Saints people had assumed. As Rona spoke at length in Arabic, tears formed in Natalie's eyes. She reached for a tissue and after a moment said, "We have to help this family." Natalie composed herself and continued. "When ISIS came to the Mousas' home, Yamo refused to convert to Islam despite fears that the women in his family might be raped. That is when his knees were broken."

"And then they had to flee somewhere else in Syria for several months?" Paul asked.

"To Damascus."

"Then when they went to Lebanon, our understanding is that they went to some sort of relative, possibly a sister-in-law?"

The three from All Saints did not follow all of Natalie's response. They gathered that the Mousa family had since moved within Lebanon, possibly in the same settlement but to a different dwelling. As the family had ended up living in an unheated attic, Rona gave them her blankets when she left for Canada.

Leandra Mousa seemed to be doing a little cleaning of houses and the church, probably in the underground economy because the Mousas were not allowed to work or access social services. Any education the children were receiving seemed to be through the church. One child may speak a little French, the second language in Lebanon, and may possibly have been learning some English.

"Do you know how their health is at the moment?" Penny asked.

"Yamo is able to walk." Natalie pulled out her smartphone and showed a photo of the eldest daughter, Elenora, bouncing in delight when she learned that Canada was likely going to be accepting them. Dressed in shorts and a tee shirt, she resembled any other thirteen year old in North America.

"I would like to help however I can," Natalie said. "I would be glad to drive to your church. Would you like to come to my home? It would be closer for the Americans. Have you ever eaten Arabic food?"

"Certainly falafel," Paul said.

"Vegetarian. Here are the phone numbers for Yamo and Leandra. I can interpret for you." This led to a side discussion between Natalie and the CLWR staff about the merits of such communications software as Viber and IMO.

"We three were born in Canada, so it's easy for us to contact our relatives," Paul said. "We don't know much about this technology." As these discussions proceeded, Rona took her own telephone and dialled the Mousas. The All Saints people stiffened, feeling surprised and unprepared, but fortunately the calls were not answered because it was the middle of the night in Lebanon.

It did not appear that Natalie was going to detail all that Rona had said about the family, especially as the conversation had its own momentum. It seemed that Natalie and her church did not expect to be involved in the settlement details. Although Natalie was eager to help the Mousa family, she was also helping others. This was an important clarification, namely that All Saints and Mount Olivet would be providing most of the support on their own, without the involvement of any other partners.

In response to Vicki's comment about housing being a major anxiety, Natalie asked, "Will housing be cheaper in your neighbourhood than where I live?"

"No, probably not. It would certainly be more convenient and would help us provide better support if the Mousas lived close to All Saints, but do you think they might want to be closer to other Syrians or an Orthodox church?"

"Oh, I'm sure they will be grateful to live anywhere that they are safe," she replied.

"That's helpful information. We've not been sure where we should begin looking for housing because we didn't know what would be the best location. It sounds like close to our church would make sense."

"If we're finished on this topic," Penny said, "could I ask something I've been wondering about?" Heads nodded in assent. "Several years ago, our church sponsored an Iraqi family. The mom and dad's English has improved and they would like to help us, as we sponsor our next family, in such ways as interpreting. We are confident of their language skills, but we also want to be sensitive whether the Mousas, as persecuted Christians, would feel comfortable having Muslims interpreting for them."

This was a potentially explosive topic, and Penny held her breath while Natalie collected her thoughts. "Are they Sunni or Shia Muslims?" Natalie asked. "Sunnis are the group that is dominant in Saudi Arabia and the majority in Syria. If they are Shia, it would probably be okay."

"I don't know. You've identified some important information for us to find out."

Paul shifted in his chair, using the armrest to pivot towards Noor. "Could you help me with timelines? My understanding is that nothing will become firm until some sort of transportation document is issued to the Mousas."

"The next step is a background check," Noor replied. "That might not be so onerous because a victimized religious minority typically doesn't pose much of a security threat to Canada. Once that's done, the medical exams will take place. After the medical exam, visas will be issued and then things should go fast. We'll keep you informed when each of these milestones is passed."

"How fast might fast be?"

"Maybe just three to five months after the medical exam."

"That's fast?"

"Yes."

"Could we write to members of parliament," Natalie interjected, "to speed up the process?"

"You could write, but remember that the Mousas are already in a priority process. They might arrive in Canada within a year, while other categories of refugees might have to wait four or five years. If they were still in Syria, it would be even slower. Canada has an office in Beirut, so that expedites things considerably."

Seeing the dejected looks, Noor continued. "The federal government announced next year's immigration targets just a few days ago. The target of 300,000 for all categories of immigrants and refugees represents almost one percent of Canada's population. The next step will be to determine the distribution across source countries. That determines how many staff will be put in each processing office. If the government decides to change staffing levels in Beirut, then the speed of issuing visas could change. The average wait times listed on the government website are not reliable anymore."

"Realistically, then," Paul said, "we should plan for an arrival no earlier than next autumn. I guess that means we should scout for housing sometime in late summer."

Oreva vigorously shook her head from side to side. "I mean," Paul backtracked, "just exploring possibilities, not signing any leases." She relaxed. "We shouldn't rent anything until the transportation forms have been issued."

"It's already a year or two since the Mousas had to flee their home," Penny said. "It's discouraging to think they may have to wait another year to get to Canada. Isn't there anything we could do for them while they're still in Lebanon?"

Noor perked up. "Perhaps a present of cash for Christmas and then a small monthly stipend."

"That makes a lot of sense to me," Paul said. "Would the money be transmitted through CLWR?"

"No," Noor replied. "The money held at our national office in Winnipeg is restricted for use only in Canada once the family arrives."

"So we'd have to raise some extra money and then send it ourselves?"

"Yes."

"Well, that strikes me as something All Saints would be pleased do. I'm not clear about the mechanics of actually sending the money."

Natalie answered, "I send money to my family through"— she hesitated—"Union?"

"Western Union?"

"That's it. I could help you to send the money through Western Union."

This seemed a good note on which to conclude the meeting, a good first step in building relationships. The group looked expectantly at each other in case anyone had another topic to raise, but nobody spoke.

"A group of us from All Saints church," Paul said, "are going next weekend to visit the two churches in Seattle. Perhaps we could contact you soon after that to arrange a call to Lebanon, take up your offer to interpret."

Natalie nodded in agreement.

"And Noor," Paul added, "I understand you'll be travelling in a week's time as well, but for a longer period."

"I am going to Kenya and Uganda, where there are many Sudanese refugees. Lutheran World Relief is hoping to settle 50,000 refugees around the world."

"Fifty thousand! All of us doing our small piece adds up to something significant."

Vicki turned towards Oreva and Noor. "Thank you for staying after office hours so we could have this meeting."

Oreva smiled in acknowledgement. "Helping people meet together to help refugees is part of what we do. It's so nice for us to see it all coming together. And thank you, Natalie and Rona, for all that you have done and will do."

The two Middle Eastern ladies stayed behind as the three from All Saints made their way to the parking lot. As they discussed when they could meet to talk about the meeting, Rona and Natalie waved goodbye as they passed by on their way to Natalie's late model Nissan.

"The sponsorship seems more real to me now," Penny said. "Until yesterday, it seemed more a concept than a reality. I'm sorry, but I can't remember how Natalie is connected. Not a sister, but a cousin or friend? The other woman was a neighbour, I understand."

"Natalie seems to be just a friend of the other woman," Vicki replied. "She didn't seem to know the Mousas at all. Once again, God seems to be bringing an unlikely group of people together. I have to admit I'm having a little difficulty, though, with the fact that the circumstances of the family are different from what we expected, especially that Natalie is not a relative. That threw me. Not that I have any problem with supporting the family in light of our current understanding. They clearly need our help."

Paul shared his thoughts. "Overall, I feel encouraged and increasingly comfortable as we gather more information and meet more people. I liked the ladies and CLWR staff. But yes, there were things I also felt uneasy about. I still don't know enough of the full story. I would have liked more of our conversation to have been translated, but I suppose that would have slowed things down considerably. Noor and Oreva have limited time, and they didn't intervene to suggest more interpretation. I felt I needed to trust their judgment and experience."

A distant car horn, carried by a light breeze along the river valley, interrupted the conversation.

"I think it's important," Penny said, "that we—the big we, including the Seattle folks—start our relationship with this family now. The earlier they get to know us, the better we can get to know them. Also, if we can start to help them financially now, no matter how much or how little, it will help to lessen the agony of the wait. At least we can feel like we're doing something."

Vicki agreed. "But I need to get going. So Wednesday night at Paul's to debrief, with Friday as the fallback if that doesn't work out?"

When she got home, she sent a quick note to Seattle. "The meeting was moving and encouraging, but also confusing, and I feel like the ground is still shifting. The three of us from All Saints need to meet and compare what we each gleaned through the language, cultural, and bureaucratic barriers—which we'll do shortly so that we have a coherent story to tell you next weekend when we begin some joint planning, to the extent we can in these early, murky days."

Seattle Bound

Before leaving All Saints in August, SRAG had invited the Canadians to Seattle in mid-autumn. Reformation Sunday, October 30, was the first suggestion, but that date would have conflicted with the launch of a yearlong celebration of the 500th anniversary of Martin Luther's posting of his ninety-five theses on the church door in Wittenberg, Germany. November 12, just four days after the American federal election, was eventually selected. In addition to visiting Mount Olivet, the Canadians would have an opportunity to learn about Benediction Church, the second church that had unexpectedly donated $5,000 to the project.

Karl proposed an agenda. "The plan is to meet around 6:00 p.m. at Benediction, conveniently just fifteen minutes from us. We'll eat there, of course. Does anyone in your group have food limitations we need to be aware of?" The next morning would include an hour-long adult forum at Mount Olivet before worship and another potluck afterwards. "Any other details we need to clarify? Greg, please correct me if I have any of this wrong."

Greg, on staff at Mount Olivet, responded promptly to say that the only change was to the adult forum on Sunday morning. "This just developed from an email I sent several months ago. The speaker I invited has now accepted." The session with Ruth Sutherland of Refugee and Asylum Services looked promising. "She and her co-workers are on the cutting edge of the effects of trauma and migration on mental health and recovery. She can identify gaps in the US system which may or may not be true in Canada."

"This all seems good to me," Paul replied. "I'm interested in what Ruth has to say—I can't imagine British Columbia has any fewer gaps—and also simply in the format of the session, as education has weakened at All Saints in recent years. And it will be nice to hear some election news from real people after all that's been in the media." Paul felt compelled to make reference to the startling election of Donald Trump as president, but respectfully decided not to mention he had yet to encounter any people in Vancouver who spoke well of the candidate's character.

Greg confirmed Paul's hunch that the election would be a significant backdrop and that some sensitivity by the Canadians would be in order. Greg wrote: "It will be an interesting weekend to say the least. I think many of us are still in shock and trying to figure out what this means policywise." He had just got off the phone with Ruth. "Her staff is anxiously wondering if Trump's promise to remove funding from sanctuary cities is a real possibility. This would affect her directly and her staff as well. I imagine both Saturday and Sunday will be a processing day, and we'll all be thankful that the family is resettling in Canada where the government is supportive of what we're all working together to do."

The Canadians began organizing transportation to Seattle. Although they quickly established that they wanted a leisurely drive with plenty of stops, virtually everything else became complicated. Somebody was coming, but then they weren't. A teenager had been missed because another person failed to communicate a message. Would an unaccompanied minor crossing the border create problems? Whose vehicles would be available, and if the owner wasn't coming, how would that affect insurance in another country? An entire Saturday morning was wasted as email exchanges eventually concluded that the seven travellers would all fit in one van, after all. It really shouldn't have been so complicated to organize, but such is the reality for volunteer organizations.

The drive to the smaller of the four border crossings in the Vancouver area took less than an hour. Because Shayla was travelling on her German passport and had encountered a complication years earlier when exiting the United States, the van was directed to a parking area on the American side and the entire group had to enter the office building of the US border service. The office was well staffed and the agents were friendly, but Shayla nonetheless spent close to fifteen minutes completing paperwork, waiting for data to be entered in the computer, and being fingerprinted. The remainder of the group felt mildly affronted by this extensive process, but Shayla was unconcerned. Once they were back in the van, she explained, "I grew up crossing the border into Communist East Germany. I'm used to intrusive border officials."

A few miles down the road, somebody suggested they stop for coffee at the little town of Lynden, a farming community with a Dutch flavour.

"What a cute place," Amelia said, the only adult member of the congregation to take up the invitation to join the trip. "I can't imagine a neater, more gracious example of small town life in North America." The first bathroom break was in Bellingham. An art store beckoned in old town Mount Vernon. Seattle was reached by mid-afternoon, leaving three or so hours to explore the park around the Space Needle just to the north of the city centre.

Right on schedule, at 5:55 p.m., the van swung into the parking lot of Benediction Lutheran church. Only one other vehicle was visible. No lights shone from the building. "Are we sure we're at the right church? Maybe there are two churches side by side in this block, and we're at the wrong one."

Shayla inched the van out of the parking lot, making a right turn to drive slowly in front of the building.

"The sign says Benediction. What's going on?" Judi asked. "I think we can pull in on the other side of the church and figure out what to do. Do we have Karl's cell number?"

As the van entered the lot on the high side of the church site, well over a dozen vehicles greeted them. Lights glowed from the windows to the left of the side entrance. All was well.

About an hour later, Karl surveyed the circular tables that each seated six to eight people. Plates looked empty and the conversation was relaxed. A couple of people were still choosing desserts at the serving table, and he suspected a teenager or two might edge back for another slice of pizza once their desserts had settled. It seemed the right time to begin the program.

He stepped to the centre of the room, microphone in hand, and gazed from table to table until he caught the attention of at least half the audience. "It's good to see faces that are familiar, even though some of us have met on only one previous occasion," he began. The noise in the room subsided. "And judging by the chatter, I'd say that many new friendships are being formed.

"Because some of us are brand new to this endeavour, I thought I'd review the origins of this project and then we could move on to learn how it was that Benediction came to be involved. Does that sound good?"

Karl waited while three or four people adjusted their chairs so they would not have to twist to see him. "It started with the news a year ago: a refugee crisis, people drowning while trying to reach Greece, horrible pictures of children and people with gunshot wounds. It was the biggest—maybe it still is—humanitarian crisis in the world at the time. My personal view is that America played a role in creating the mess in the Middle East, and we should take at least some responsibility for the consequences. Maybe I'm misguided, but that's how I see it."

Karl collected his thoughts and continued. "William and I didn't see any easy way to make a difference by working through channels in the United States—granted, we didn't look that hard and perhaps we should have been more creative. It seemed, however, like a lane was wide open in Canada because the prime minister was welcoming refugees with open arms. 'That's great,' I said to William, 'we can be part of that.'

"I did some internet research and reached out to Canadian Lutheran World Relief, saying, 'I see you sponsor refugee families. Can we help with that? Do you want some money?'" He glanced at some of his friends from Mount Olivet. "I figured everybody wants money, right?"

Glances were exchanged and faces lit up with smiles. Karl let the Mount Olivet people savour the moment.

"After a few follow-up phone calls," he said, "Noor at Canadian Lutheran World Relief put me in contact with Pastor Ellen Thompson. I shanghaied Greg from our church, and we all met in Seattle over a beer. The rest is history. We had a great initial meeting with Pastor Ellen and her friend, the bishop from Edmonton."

"There were some small world occurrences," Greg interjected. "The bishop's husband and my dad went to seminary together in Saskatchewan. It was very symbiotic."

"Yes," Karl agreed. "We had a good conversation and then things sort of took off. At that point, we founded SRAG and started raising money. The money poured in very quickly. We had $10,000 or $12,000 within a couple of weeks.

"Pastor Ellen went to her group at All Saints, and they had some questions and deliberations, but they gave an affirmative response. Things just kept happening. It all happened very quickly, very naturally, and so here we are tonight."

Judi waved her left arm. "I wasn't going to ask because I thought it too crass. But since you mentioned that everybody wants money, how did you conduct your fundraising campaign? It was remarkably effective."

Karl shook his head and shrugged his shoulders. "There was no big fundraising campaign. Just word of mouth, first within the church and then beyond to friends. People responded very generously without a lot of strong-arm tactics. Sometimes upon hearing of the project, the donor took the initiative by saying, 'How can I help?' or 'Here's a cheque.' It went faster and easier than expected. We were fundraising without even knowing what particular family we would be helping." He added, as if an afterthought, "Church council wasn't all that involved. They mainly watched and said 'Go for it.'"

Now it was Paul who had a question. "So you're zipping along, money coming in faster and easier than you ever expected. In the meantime, All Saints is deliberating and dawdling and taking forever to decide if it wants to get involved. What was it like for you, having to wait at a distance and wondering if we would become partners or not?"

"Honestly," Karl replied, "we weren't too concerned whether All Saints might decline because we figured we could easily find another Canadian congregation if that happened. We just kept on fundraising."

Greg spoke up. "There were forty-two donations totalling a little over $27,000 American. Benediction's $5,000 raised the number of donors to forty-three."

"It's a good chunk of change," concluded Karl, "that's now held in trust, awaiting the family's arrival." He made eye contact with a woman standing at the back. She nodded and Karl continued. "Alison from Benediction has to run, but I wanted us all to hear what brought Benediction into this partnership."

Alison moved to the front of the room and took the microphone from Karl. "Five of us are here tonight representing Benediction," she began. "None of us prepared a talk, so what I am about to say is ad lib and moved by the Holy Spirit."

"You fit right in with the rest of us," a voice called out.

"Our involvement started with our church leadership. Evelyn Knowlton, who is an administrator on staff, and our pastor, Francine, approached our endowment committee about the possibility of a grant for the refugee project. The endowment, which some members started in 1989, provides gifts that are being used locally, nationally, and throughout the world. Our committee, and I guess our church generally, is always looking for things of service to do.

"If we can set an example by helping one family, by making a difference in just one family, with our Canadian brothers and sisters up North, then we hope somehow we'll come to be able to do more in the United States. Collaboration, especially in these tough times, is about the smile, the look in the eyes, seeing Christ in another individual, and looking beyond, finding a light. The family from Syria really needs us. They'll probably never meet some of us, but at least we know we've done our part. One family at a time. It's hard for us to get our arms around all the issues in the world."

Alison passed the microphone back to Karl. He said, "I'll take the liberty of speaking for everybody here. Thank you, Benediction, because your gift of $5,000 literally fell from the sky. It was exactly what we needed, exactly when we needed it, and it's going to make a huge difference. It's such a joy to add you to our partnership. We have our friends from Canada, our friends across I-90, and now at Benediction. We're all in this together. It's great to be here today.

"And now some housekeeping. Greg, could you come forward to help organize the homestays and remind us of the schedule for tomorrow?"

Refugee 101

Upholstered office partitions at the far end of the Mount Olivet church hall created an intimate but flexible space for the hour-long adult class that met most Sundays before the worship service.

With the seemingly inevitable technical problems of connecting the speaker's notebook computer to the church's portable projector finally resolved, Mike Doucette called the group to order. He introduced the speaker, Ruth Sutherland, and welcomed the guests, "some from across the border in Canada and some from across the water of Lake Washington." He dispensed with further preliminaries because the session was already behind schedule.

Ruth smiled at the audience of three dozen and stepped forward to begin her talk. "As Mike mentioned, I work locally with refugees and asylum seekers. My first slide gives you an overview of the services we provide:

- Unaccompanied refugee minor program, which is primarily about orphaned refugee children
- Mental health program, primarily for PTSD and depression, with about 600 clients
- Survivors of torture program that has served 700 people from 66 different countries in the last four years
- Complex medical program for newcomers to the United States who have a serious medical condition—such as a child with cerebral palsy or a cancer diagnosis, or HIV—to help them navigate our bewildering medical system
- Asylum services program

"I'm not going to describe these, but feel free at the end to ask any questions.

"What I want to do today is give you a quick Refugee 101 lesson. In the United States, and probably in Canada, all newcomers were simply considered immigrants until 1951. There was no special class of immigration for refugees. In other words, we took in refugees but we didn't call them that.

"As information about the full horror of the Holocaust emerged following World War II, a special track was created in 1951 for immigrants with humanitarian concerns. The UN High

Commissioner for Refugees came to define a refugee as someone who is outside their country of origin and cannot return for grave fear of persecution." She looked away from the slide. "What do you see as the key points in this definition?"

A significant number of eyes broke contact with Ruth. Eventually, an elderly man gave a tentative answer. "If you're inside your country of origin, you are not technically considered a refugee. You have to be outside."

"Exactly," Ruth said. "Now here's the other important point. Refugees must have a humanitarian claim. It can't just be an economic problem or famine, or a desire for a better life. The claimant must not be able to return home for grave fear of persecution or harm from others."

"Outside your country, and people at home making it unsafe for you to return," the same man interjected. "That's what makes you a refugee."

"Exactly again," Ruth said. "Refugees flee to a second country. They may be encamped there or they may be in exile, which is the term for an urban refugee who is registered with the UN but not in a camp. Right now, two-thirds of refugees are urban and not in a camp. They're all in a holding pattern, waiting to be officially allowed into a new country, by no means expecting it might be the one they're currently in."

Ruth clicked the remote and accidentally scrolled through three slides. She backtracked too far, but eventually found the slide about asylum seekers that she wanted.

"Asylum seekers are different. They get to their destination country first and then file a humanitarian claim. In Canada, I think the equivalent terminology is refugee claimant and the process may be different. In any event, in America, a judge decides if the claim is valid. If valid, they can come in as an asylee, which is similar to refugee status. If not, they normally get deported.

"In contrast to asylees, all refugees come into the US papered, able to work, with all their security clearances and medical clearances done. Everything happens overseas and then they arrive." She let the point sink in. "Refugees are not part of our undocumented or illegal immigrant problem.

"Finally, in addition to refugees and asylum seekers, there is another type of displacement. Internally displaced people, or IDPs, are people who have fled their homes but are still within their country of origin. If you have to flee Damascus to another city, you're still under the sovereignty of Syria. Whatever sort of humanitarian aid you receive largely depends on the permission of the country of sovereignty. If aid workers are not invited in by the government, they enter at their peril."

Ruth stared emphatically at her audience. "The next slide is heartbreaking. We are currently experiencing the biggest surge of displaced people since the end of World War II. In 2014, the latest year for which we have statistics, one out of every 122 humans in the world was either a refugee, an internally displaced person, or seeking asylum. It's really saddening. That's over 65 million people who have been displaced from their homes."

"That's about twice the population of Canada," Paul called out.

"Question," a young woman said to Ruth. "I don't know if you can answer this, but how well do we do here compared to others in helping these people?"

Ruth thought for a moment. This was a broad question that could be answered in a number of different ways. Finally she responded. "Washington State has historically been a very welcoming environment for refugees. At the end of the Vietnam War, many states closed their borders to refugees, including what we consider to be liberal California. The governor of California made that state a hostile place for the boat people. The Washington governor, on the other hand, said, 'We want them in Washington. They will be assets to our communities. We ask businesses and individuals to step up and welcome people.' And they did." The young woman looked pleased.

"Any other questions before I continue?"

"Who decides where they settle?"

"That's a really great question," Ruth said, "because it's different in Canada than the United States. In the US, all refugees get connected to one of the country's nine refugee resettlement agencies. Each year, each office in each agency will say what settlement capacity they believe they currently have. That data goes back to DC. Unless the refugee has a strong tie with a particular region in the country, the agencies just disperse the refugees wherever."

Ruth glanced at her watch and scrolled through half a dozen slides, this time intentionally. "Our time is limited, so I'm going to skip some sections of this presentation to make sure I get to the parts that Greg suggested last week would be of particular interest to you."

She shifted her weight onto her left leg and continued speaking. "In the mental health field, we typically think about the three stages of being a refugee: first, the fleeing, and then the encampment or exile, and finally, the resettlement. Fleeing is generally the most violent stage. You can imagine what it would take for you to leave your home, your job, your neighbours, your community, your credentials, and everything you own, never to return. Normally, what makes people walk away is that they fear for their life or, even more commonly, they fear for their children's lives.

"The vast majority of refugees are children. They are a huge motivator for parents. Adults without children are more apt to stick around a little longer and see how things go. They think they can hide more easily and flee more easily. When you have children, that really shifts your thinking and motivates people to get out of their country.

"Turning now to encampment or exile, this can also be a time of trauma. Even if people are encamped, the conditions aren't great.

Camps are set up to be temporary, but in fact, the average time people spend in a refugee camp is seventeen years. The processing time is a little quicker for Syrians right now, but it's not uncommon for me to have people coming from camps in Kenya or Thailand after more than twenty years there."

People in the audience exchanged glances. They were receiving some staggering, and disturbing, numbers.

"Camps can be very dangerous places. They're often raided by the locals for child trafficking or to create child soldiers. But if you're in exile, it can be even more difficult. In some of the camps that have been around for a while, they at least have education and health care. When you're out in the urban area, you don't get any of that. It's really perilous.

"It's no surprise that these folks have higher rates of poor mental health. About one-third of refugees and asylum seekers will have some sort of mental health diagnosis. Their rate of PTSD is about ten times that of the general population. It's not because of weakness or character defects. It's generally because of the trauma they've been through.

"But that's not the important point. Rather, two-thirds don't have a diagnosis, which I find a huge surprise. They've been through war, through trauma. They've been displaced from their home country, but they do not have any mental health diagnosis. I think that really speaks to the resilience of the people we work with.

"Most of the reasons people develop depression is external stressors and loss. Most of the reasons people develop PTSD is trauma, and that is 'dose dependent': intensity, frequency, and duration. It's not a surprise that you get a lot of this stuff among refugees."

Sensing that Ruth had come to the end of this section, Paul waited a moment and, not hearing anyone else speak, raised his hand. "I'd like to make a comment that fits somewhere between mental health and homesickness. My daughter told me of a conversation she had with a federal government employee in Canada who had been hired temporarily to help with the influx of Syrian refugees. The government caught a family that had slipped through the cracks, entering Canada falsely as refugees by lying about where they'd been and what they'd done in the Middle East. Although liars, they weren't horrible people just because they wanted to come to Canada for a better life rather than because they'd been hurt or persecuted in Syria.

"What's significant is that they were not doing well in Canada. They were having trouble adjusting because the transition into a new culture had been too quick. It seems that the waiting refugees have in camps or in exile gives them time to process their losses, to grieve, so to speak. Those who have been disconnected from their homes and loved ones for a longer period are apparently more ready to move on with their lives and adapt to their new country. The waiting may be harsh medicine, but maybe it serves a purpose. In any event, it's helped me to better appreciate the complexities of setting refugee policy."

Somebody cleared their throat, another person shifted in their chair, but mostly the audience remained still. They were starting to feel the human impact of displacement in a far deeper way than any set of statistics could convey. Greg thought of the scheduling obstacles he had faced in organizing this session and was grateful he'd not simply given up. God's spirit seemed to be at work.

Ruth resumed. "As a refugee, you really only have three choices, you know. You can return home, you can be absorbed into the country you're in (which most countries don't make easy), or you can be resettled. We in America and Canada think mainly in terms of resettled refugees, but the blunt reality is that less than one-half of one percent of refugees will ever get the opportunity to resettle, to start their life over in a new country.

"Now think about your second choice as a refugee, namely the possibility of returning home when the conflict is over. Yes, returning to the home country can and does happen, but look at how long the conflict has been going on in Somalia, in Iraq, in Afghanistan. If you're from those countries and you're waiting to return home, you're probably stuck for a very long period.

"So what about the country you're currently in, the third option? Well, most countries the refugees are in are not saying 'Bring me your tired, your poor, and we will welcome them with open arms.' Frankly, they don't want those displaced people. They generally just say, 'You can stay, but you cannot affect the local economy. You can't get jobs, you can't go to school, you can't get medicine. We're going to give you the worst land. We're going to wall you off in an encampment and not let you leave so that you're not competing with the locals.'

"Imagine living in a region that at best just barely tolerates you and more probably resents you. You endure, you suffer, and you wait. That's life for most refugees."

Ruth looked at Karl. "When we chatted before the session, you asked if I could say a few words about the process by which refugees get into this country."

"Yes," Karl replied, "but I didn't realize then that I was asking about less than one percent."

"Yes, they're a small proportion, but they're the real people you and I encounter. These next slides touch on them, at least from an American perspective.

"Each September, a presidential determination sets a refugee quota for the coming year and identifies which countries they will come from. This year, the number was about 125,000 from thirty-three countries. Next year, the new president will decide whether to take in any refugees or not. And if so, from which countries.

"The role of Congress is to allocate funding to support whatever number the president comes up with. Two years ago when refugees became such a hot button issue, as if it were a new thing, Congress decided to disburse federal dollars quarterly. The next quarterly vote will be in December. So even if the presidential determination stands, there may be no money for refugee resettlement in just a matter of weeks."

"Even before the new government takes office?" came a question from the same young woman who had spoken before.

"I can't say for sure," Ruth said. "I just know that, in conversations with the State Department this past Wednesday, they said they'll continue resettling through December but then they don't know what will happen. It's a significant, profound period of uncertainty, and it has already started.

"I'm staggered by the misinformation that started appearing two years ago. The numbers being thrown about were along the lines of 250,000 Syrians entering the country and that we didn't know where they were coming from. Here's a graph that gives you the real facts. It shows the number of refugees from all countries entering the US from 1980 to 2016.

"The news media is portraying hordes of refugees entering the United States, but really, we've plateaued since 2001, with a slight uptick in recent years. After the fall of Saigon, we had about 240,000 refugees in 1980. The number dropped in subsequent years, and then there was a spike after the fall of the Soviet Union. This year the quota is 125,000. Nothing unusual is happening by historical standards.

"Nothing, nada." Ruth pushed back her hair behind her ears and looked at her notes. "Sorry, I get a bit ticked about the misinformation. Let me get back to describing the process.

"After the president determines the ceiling, the State Department meets with the UN High Commissioner for Refugees—and with other countries, because countries tend to do things in consortia— to plan the logistics of resettling refugees. While this occurs, refugees go in and register.

"If the claimants meet the humanitarian criteria, they have about six security checks. If they pass those, then they wait, and they wait, and they wait for their number to come up. If their number comes up, they get more security checks—so now they're up to about nine—and they get a medical check for communicable diseases. Both the security and the medical must be current, within six months, before people are allowed into the United States. After they get here, they will have medical checks again. The government considers it very important to protect the US from communicable diseases.

"Travel is arranged through the international office for migration. The airfares, incidentally, are a loan. In the US, newcomers get billed six months after arriving. They are received in the US by a settlement agency that provides ninety days of casework assistance. The settlement agency helps connect them to employment and ESL, registers kids in school, and helps them apply for a social security number. Refugees are mandated to have another medical check upon arrival here, mostly for communicable diseases, and the agencies help them find a primary care provider.

"The agency also helps them rent an apartment in market-rate housing, not in low-income or subsidized housing. People will say that refugees get things that nobody else gets, but that's not true. Refugees compete for market-rate housing just like everybody else.

"Often people are very strapped for money, and often they're homesick as well. Remember that, whereas many people are pulled to the US, refugees are generally pushed. They're pushed out of their countries. Many of them had good, successful lives in their country, but they've been pushed to have to leave.

"So that's the refugee process in a nutshell. Let me talk now for a few moments about the other group, about asylum seekers." Normally the audience would have wiggled and flexed at a transition point such as this, but today it remained focused. One late arriver unobtrusively slipped into a chair on the edge.

"The first question is why do we even have asylum seekers? The answer is that we don't take in refugees from every country. Remember the presidential determination not only sets a quota but specifies sources. We don't take refugees from, say, Liberia or Sierra Leone, Tibet or El Salvador. If you run afoul of the government in Tibet, if you are a Christian in China, if you are a political activist in Haiti, the only way to get protection in the United States is to get here first and then ask for protection. That's what an asylum claim is.

"Last year, we had 25,000 people granted asylum in the US. It's been as low as a couple of thousand and as high as 40,000, depending on the year. It's a rather arbitrary process. It depends on the judge—it's not a jury—and if you're in South Texas, the numbers are abysmally low, say ten percent. In this area of Seattle, they can be around forty percent. It's very much based on the political climate and the judge who's deciding your case. People's personal beliefs can come into the decisions they make.

"Asylum seekers have no right to legal counsel, even for children. If you're lucky, you'll get a pro bono lawyer. When you ask for asylum, the first officer you meet can decide whether or not they think you even have a claim. If they don't think you have a claim, they can move to deport you right then. There's no oversight on that; they just get to decide. If they believe you might possibly have a claim, they'll give you a list of lawyers you can contact for representation. There's only one organization in Washington State that provides pro bono legal services for immigration cases. They get 1,100 to 1,500 calls a week for service.

"Or you can try to find somebody that you can pay. If you happen to be well resourced, like some of the people from Turkey right now where it's many judges and doctors and such are being rounded up, then you may have some money to do that.

"Even if you are on community release, you as an asylum seeker cannot access any benefits until you actually file for asylum. It can take up to a year to get your legal case prepared. Even then, the only benefit you're eligible for is Washington State food stamps, $135 a month in food. You can petition the US government to work in 180 days, but it may not be granted. The average asylum seeker who is not in detention is going to wait eighteen months before they can work. During that time, they really can't access any benefits except food stamps. So it's a very vulnerable population and one that we often see gets trafficked after they get here."

Ruth clicked the remote. Only one word appeared on the next slide: Questions.

She asked the audience what else was on their minds. Several hands shot up. "How about you?" she asked, pointing to the far left. "I fear I had my back to you too often, so let me make up by having you go first."

"No, you didn't," the gentleman replied, "but I'm happy to go first anyhow. I'm curious how your organization is funded to support refugees once they get here. I'm wondering whether you will be able to continue at least some of your work regardless of any new federal policies."

Ruth thought for a moment. "About two-thirds of the funding for resettlement in the US is federal. They're called reception and placement funds. The agencies raise money to supplement that funding. Should all federal money go away, I don't know if the agencies could raise enough to replace it.

"Some of our programs, such as our complex medical program, are mostly state funded, but even some of this block money ultimately comes from the feds. The service suite that I work in is about seventy percent federally funded. There are people who are trying to assure me that nothing is really going to change due to the election and that everything will be okay. It would be nice if they're right, but that's not a foregone conclusion in the worsening political climate.

"Here's an example of the climate. In the nearby city where our offices are located, we found out last year that the city manager was mapping every Muslim home in the city in case there was a terrorist incident and they wanted to find Muslims quickly. Now granted, he was let go after this initiative came to light. But imagine how this affected the forty percent of the staff where I work who are Muslim.

"Furthermore, there are many profound intersections in these refugee communities. People don't sit in just one community. Many of the people who we serve are not only Muslim but also black. Or maybe an asylum seeker is LGBTQ, coming from a country where they could be jailed or killed for their sexual orientation. We just had a transgender client from Russia who had been put in a psych ward for three years because they were considered mentally ill. So it's not just refugees or people of colour or people marginalized by their sexual orientation. Some people face multiple challenges.

"But I digress, and I see there are plenty of other questions. I'll sum up by saying there's two risks to resettlement. One is that the government closes the pipeline and won't allow any more refugees in. The second is that federal funding is pulled."

Vicki half stood from her chair to catch Ruth's attention. "I want to go back to your comment about the uncertainty. Are organizations speaking up? Are groups like the Lutheran denomination taking a stand?"

Ruth shrugged her shoulders. "Honestly, I think it's caught a lot of people flat-footed. People are still scrambling, even on our end. All the settlement agencies have said they will work with the Trump administration for fair policies. They are calling on him to continue America's historic and longstanding commitment to accepting refugees and providing humanitarian protection. Nothing has been proposed yet, nor any action taken.

"Right now, we're mainly trying to assure our clients and staff that they're safe. There's tremendous fear. Already people are beginning to experience significant hate crimes. Our first step has been to let them know that our organizations are allies to their safety. For example, groups are putting together tool kits for dealing with bullying in schools.

"I don't know what the landscape in the United States is going to look like for newcomers next year. Is all this extreme talk about shutting down the refugee program just campaign rhetoric? Or are some refugees going to be let in but with restrictive vetting, such as a religious litmus test that only lets in Christians? Or will things stay much the same? This uncertainty makes it hard for me to tell folks like you how you can help.

"We do know that refugees still have an avenue of safety into Canada, so contributing money there helps. Fighting for policy changes here."

William interjected, "So how do you not despair?"

Ruth may have been tempted to gloss over this question, to treat it as a throwaway comment, but she chose to take it seriously. After a long pause, she said slowly, "I'm so tired. I don't know. I've been sick, just sick."

She swallowed, stared at the ceiling for a moment, and then scanned the audience. "One ray of hope comes to me from my experience of working with refugees and asylum seekers for over a decade. I'm so buoyed by the resilience of the people I serve, and their ability not only to survive but to still love." The room was silent.

"That's the thing," she continued carefully. "People can be so beaten down, but they still have the ability to love and show compassion. To form meaningful relationships and still have something to give. It has always made me feel that, instead of slogging at work or seeing something that felt like a tragedy, my job inspires me. I see people with nothing, absolutely nothing, who still have the capacity to give. It makes me want to be a better person."

She bit her lip and then took a deep breath. "It's so hard for me to feel right now that the people I value and love, and take as an inspiration, have been anything but negated. They're at risk." Her voice wavered. "I'll probably be fine if I lose my job. I can get another one. But that doesn't mean that the people I care about are safe. For the first time ever, I am honestly struggling between despair and active resistance.

"It's not that I don't believe in the legitimacy of the election," she continued in a more animated manner, "but I will resist every policy, every action that attempts to negate the people who I believe make America great, who increase our capacity to be better people, and who help us strive towards a more equal country. This truly is what I believe America is about and what makes us rich. It is everything that I am."

She remained silent for ten seconds. Finally, she shrugged and spoke softly. "So…that's all I can say. I vacillate between extreme despair and action. I think, whatever happens, it's going to be a long haul for everybody."

She breathed evenly and then smiled weakly. "What other questions do you people have as I step off my soapbox?"

Shayla stood so that her voice would project. "What do you think of the UN High Commissioner for Refugees' desire to give cash funding to refugees who haven't been resettled, like Syrians who are trapped in Jordan and Lebanon? To give them monthly cash payments. Is that an avenue for people to become involved?"

Ruth rubbed her chin. "I don't know a lot about this proposal, but I know the vast majority of refugees will never be resettled. I do think there needs to be some sort of move along these lines because of the prolonged time when displaced people have to find ways to eat and pay rent. So without knowing the specifics, it seems on the surface like a good one to me."

Next to speak was a middle-aged woman. She brushed aside a strand of greying hair and said, "In August, I was in Minnesota for a reunion and saw three highrises that stood out from their surroundings. My friend said disparagingly, 'That's where the Somalis are.' This is an intelligent, well-travelled woman, yet what I heard and saw left me discouraged. The buildings looked like projects: decrepit, with curtains blowing out windows. The buildings used to belong to the university and used to have beautiful gardens.

"I asked how so many Somalis came to be in this place. She said, 'The churches brought them. They're not integrating into the community. They work at the lowest paying jobs or don't work at all.'

"My question is, what is your experience of your clients becoming integrated into our society?"

"If you look at who has come as refugees since 1951," Ruth replied, "Vietnamese, Cambodian, Ethiopian, Russian, Ukrainian, Croatian...how many groups would you say have not become a part of the fabric of this community? Don't we think of these people now as American?

"Yes, the first generation always finds it difficult. Think of the people you know who say their grandmother never learned to speak English, but the next generation absolutely became American. They don't have a choice. The next generation learns English and becomes integrated into our society."

Ruth looked to her left and many eyes followed her gaze. "I see Mike and Greg huddled together," she said. "I suspect they're getting anxious because our time is more than up and the church service is probably going to start in about seven seconds. So off you go. I don't need a special closing or thanking. Just having had you here, listening and caring at this time in American history, has made this session more than worthwhile for me. Blessings upon us all."

"I wish I had heard this talk six months ago," Paul said to Shayla as they made their way out. "I learned a lot."

Next Steps

"It's refreshing to worship at a new place where I feel so at home," Judi said as she ambled across the lawn from the sanctuary to Mount Olivet's hall.

"Refreshing and novel," Amelia replied. "I liked the inclusive language. I was halfway through the Lord's Prayer before I realized that's what it was."

Twenty minutes later, with everybody well through lunch, Karl rose with a microphone in hand. "This seems a good time to start some conversation. In particular, we need to decide which of the good ideas we touched on last night we should act upon.

"Then we'll have to decide who will be involved. For example, the Skype call to the family in Lebanon. We can't all be on the call. And if we decide to provide a monthly stipend, I have no idea how much they need. Is it $10 or $100?" He noticed some motion. "Shayla, do you want to say something?"

Shayla nodded. "The UN High Commissioner for Refugees has a program where refugees receive monthly cash stipends. I'd like to contact them to see if they have something similar in Lebanon. I believe they suggested $167 Canadian is enough in much of the world to support a family of six for a month."

"It's not a lot of money," Karl commented. "Any other questions or observations to help us deal with this list of ideas? Volunteers? Yes, what's on your mind, Cynthia?"

"I love the Christmas parcel idea, but if there is a Skype call, I hope we can find out whether it's stuff or money that's appropriate— probably money, because it's more flexible. A stipend gives them a source of income."

"As somebody pointed out earlier," Karl elaborated, "Christmas is probably Orthodox Christmas, two weeks later than ours. We'd also have to check the reliability of postal delivery in Lebanon."

An older lady caught Karl's eye. "We used to send parcels to Liberia with packages of M&M candies on top. The government people would take the candy but the parcels got through. We'll have to ensure that whatever we do, we don't somehow penalize these people in how they are viewed by their peers or others."

Shayla took her turn to speak. "Sometimes the sponsorship doesn't work out for whatever reason, say, medical or security. In fact, some sponsorship groups have been asked to change families simply because the second family was ready to come right away." Shayla could feel the energy in the room drop as people considered her comment. "Sorry to be a wet blanket, but if we think these things through now, we can minimize disappointments and problems in the future."

"You're right," Lori-Ann said. She lived some distance from Mount Olivet church but was keenly involved. "And it would be even more dislocating and disappointing for the refugee family. But I still think it's worth making contact, especially given the encouragement by the CLWR folks to do so. If at some point the family switches, we could switch our efforts to the new family. We committed to bringing a family here, not some particular group of individuals."

Karl waited to see if anybody else wanted to speak. Seeing none, he said, "Just to start closing the loops, it sounds like everybody's excited about the possibility of a Skype call. Lori-Ann, did I just hear you volunteer to be on that call?"

"Smoothly done, Karl. Yes, if I can and it works out. I have a work schedule."

"Of course," Karl said. "Are there any other Seattle people who would be interested in joining Lori-Ann? I don't actually know how to dial-in additional people, but maybe some young kids could help us. The video conferencing technology is out there for this to happen." He looked around. "You, too, William. Are you interested?"

"If scheduling works out."

"Let's not hold up a simple phone call the Vancouver guys can easily make because of us in Seattle," Lori-Ann suggested. "Just make contact through whatever means you can and get the information. Then, if we can, schedule something with Skype for more of us to join in. The important first step is to make contact, not to have all of us there."

"And during that call, we can begin to find out what they need or want in terms of Christmas and so on," Karl summarized. "Let's turn our attention to a photo album. I've already collected some pictures, and there's a bunch of new pictures from this weekend. I'm not the most artsy person. So I wonder if somebody would help me put them into an album that we could either share with them electronically or print up hard copies to mail to them? I'll work with you on that."

Karl wanted to keep the meeting moving. "Looking ahead to the family's arrival, it's too early to do any concrete planning because it may be a year from now. So let me ask the Canadians, is there anything in your mind that we can be doing collectively to prepare for their arrival?"

The Canadians sat back in their chairs. Finally, Judi grinned and said, "How about learning some Arabic? Just a basic vocabulary of a hundred words."

"I won't speak for others," Karl said, "but that is a rather, uh, challenging idea for me. Worthwhile, to be sure, but challenging."

"I was only semi-serious," Judi said. "Perhaps if you can find a place locally to step in and help, and thereby learn about Middle Eastern culture, that would go a long ways towards becoming more educated. And you'd feel like you're doing something useful while we're waiting."

"I have a story about learning a few foreign phrases," said a woman on the other side of the room. "We waited at the airport for a ten-year-old girl to arrive from Korea. We had learned some words of Korean to welcome her, but our pronunciation was off. We thought that we were saying 'beautiful' as she arrived, but it was really 'sick.' Oh, well."

Karl chuckled. "That's funny. We're bound to make mistakes. Any other thoughts, feelings, or questions?"

An older lady took the microphone. "I have a large extended family, and I give various amounts of money to them at Christmas.

If I asked at our Christmas party whether any would like to give part of their gift to our family, I know they would. I think there are other people who would want to be a part of this."

"Great idea."

Lori-Ann spoke again. "I was thinking about the stipend. Maybe it could be organized in a way where everyone takes on a month, say, each family taking on $125 a month. Or two families."

"Another great idea," Karl agreed. "That way we'd only make one ask. We wouldn't have to go scrambling every month." He scanned the room, looking for others who might want to speak.

"I have a tiny practical detail," Vicki said. "Who will be our main Seattle contacts?"

"Up until now," Karl replied, "it's been Greg and me. As you know, Greg will be leaving his job in February. I don't know if he'll continue being involved with this. We'll let you know."

"If you need someone else as an interim contact, I'm glad to do that," Lori-Ann volunteered.

"That was easy," someone murmured.

"Let's exchange an email and phone list," Lori-Ann suggested. "I'll get some paper."

"I'll send an email to people who aren't here and invite them to sign up as well," Karl said.

Paul stood and turned to face the entire group. "A comment. You're frequently, constantly, asking, 'How can we help?' Don't underestimate how much you've already done. Not just the fundraising, but in terms of getting our church to do something. None of this would have happened without you. The constant encouragement, the constant rejoicing, the sharing back and forth. There's a lot of wonderful things happening. All Saints is feeling very well supported. Just thank you so much for what you have done and continue to do."

"It's mutual, I think," Karl replied. "If we've concluded our business, well, I guess we can just start cleaning up."

Connecting with Lebanon

Two weeks after their visit to Seattle, the Vancouver group began planning their first call to the Mousa family in Lebanon. Even something this simple involved coordinating schedules and ensuring the availability of an interpreter. December 15 was proposed, but Shayla was about to depart for the North Pole (briefly, at 33,000 feet, on her way to Germany) and two others wanted to attend a Candlelight and Carols service that evening. Eventually a date was chosen to meet at Shayla's home.

Vicki volunteered to give Zrebar a ride—the team was unsure whether it was culturally acceptable for Zrebar to ride alone with a male who was not a relative—but it snowed just sufficiently to snarl traffic so the meeting was cancelled. Vicki used the time to research the cost of sending a parcel to Lebanon. "It appears that the cheapest by Canada Post would be about $102 and would take one to three months. That's by international parcel service. A priority worldwide parcel would be—get ready for this—$240." The lack of a Lebanese postal code prevented her from checking the cost of a private service such as UPS.

The video call was finally made on December 14. Shayla told the early arrivers to make themselves welcome while she and her husband dashed off separately for fifteen minutes to transport their children to different events. Of the seven adults who eventually appeared—four from All Saints, Zrebar, Natalie and her husband—only two had been born in Canada.

The All Saints contingent was unclear whether the Christian Syrians would normally have met in a social situation with a Muslim Iraqi, but they hoped this occasion might be another way of building bridges and understanding. Zrebar's headscarf seemed to take the others aback when she entered the room, but the five or so years she had spent as a displaced person in several locations in Syria proved a helpful icebreaker.

December 16, 2016
Paul's summary of the video call for SRAG:

> I'd characterize the phone call as joyous chaos. It was about 5:00 a.m. in Lebanon, but Yamo and Leandra woke their three kids—bleary and bewildered—to join in the call. There was plenty of waving and smiling, images jerking from person to person, and a few moments when the transmission froze. Just the opposite of slick choreography or formal introductions. In many ways, it resembled phone calls that will be made all over the world on Christmas, including a Christmas tree in their background.
>
> Our family is currently living with a sister who married a Lebanese. The kids are able to attend school in the afternoon after the Lebanese children have finished. The little bit of second language that at least one child is learning is French—of limited, but some, value in this part of Canada.
>
> We agreed on a secret question they'd have to answer when we wire money. Our local Western Union is in a payday loan office. The transfer on Thursday went quickly and smoothly, and many details about the sender and recipient will be saved in their system to simplify the next transfer we make.

Lori-Ann was the first from Seattle to respond to the update. "Hallelujah! This is wonderful and thank you for sharing it so eloquently. Here's to joyous chaos!"

Shayla wrote, "I'm kind of out of time before my trip but want to say I felt there were incredible things happening during this phone call. Natalie said the Mousa family is going to church and will be lighting a candle in gratitude and appreciation of our congregation." She closed by saying she would try to contact the local member of Parliament in early January in the hope of speeding up the application process.

The electronic discussion concluded with Penny writing "This family adds an extra level of meaning as we read Scripture in the coming days about no room at the inn."

Christmas came and went, with Penny paying particular attention to Matthew's account of the Holy Family's flight to escape Herod's slaughter of babies whose mere existence might incite insurrection. Conflict and occupying forces in the Middle East. Fleeing one's country to protect a child. *That's a classic refugee story,* she mused. *Good thing Egypt accepted refugees. I wonder if that's why Mary and Joseph were led south rather than north to what is now Lebanon. Or maybe their destination had something to do with the extent of Herod's jurisdiction. I wish we'd been told what it was like being in exile in Egypt.*

Four weeks had passed since SRAG received news from Canada. They didn't want to be nags, nor did they doubt that All Saints would promptly share important information, but SRAG was losing momentum. It was hard to know exactly what they should do next to support the Mousa family while in Lebanon. A tactful enquiry was in order.

Yvonne sent the email. "I'm part of the Mount Olivet/Seattle refugee resettlement committee, and I have a question. Two families here have each contributed $100 that we would like to somehow be used for our family for monthly support as they and we await their arrival in Canada. I understand that you guys have a way to get money to them." She asked whether to send the money to All Saints church or to somebody on the welcoming team. "We're eager to hear what, if anything, is happening, and if they're all right."

Paul responded right away, feeling sheepish that All Saints was not more proactive. "We learned on our first transfer that we can only send US not Canadian dollars to Lebanon. I'll ask at my bank tomorrow if there's a way for us to cash a US cheque directly into US currency without having the service charges of converting it in and out of Canadian currency. We may have to do something complicated this time and work out a more streamlined process for the future."

He noted it would be simpler for the money to go straight from Seattle to Lebanon, instead of routing it through Canada. However, that would mean coordinating payments from the two groups so there would be no gaps or duplication. "Also, until we've had more communication with our family and are sure they understand all that's going on, we need to minimize the number of people they deal with."

"I have some concerns about our sending money directly," Yvonne said, "and feel it would be easier to manage things without double monthly assistance sent by accident if those funds could be sent by your group." She emphasized that her crowd was not interested in tax deductions or personal recognition. "I don't want to make work for you guys or complicate things in any way. This is not a huge amount of money and I don't want to make it harder than it's worth." She was curious, though, what the Canadians thought would be an appropriate amount to send each month and what the fees would be.

Paul responded to Yvonne a couple of days later to confirm his bank could cash an American cheque in Canada and give him American cash. "The fees Western Union charges to wire money are inescapable: $15 to send $100, $17 for $200, $23 for $400, and so on. In December, I went in with $250 Canadian. After fees and currency conversion, our family received $180 US, if memory serves me well. I don't know how much they lose when converting US dollars to the local currency, or whether Lebanon is one of those countries where shops sometimes accept American money."

The welcoming team scheduled a meeting at Vicki's home to decide the frequency and amount of money to send to the Mousas. Before the group could get together, however, Vicki had to leave to attend her brother-in-law's funeral in Manitoba so the location of the meeting needed to change. Paul said he was happy to host the meeting. "But if those with more complicated family schedules than mine would prefer a different location, please speak up."

Shayla's family schedule was indeed complicated. She proposed meeting instead at a coffee shop closer to her home. Judi missed the meeting to help her husband look for his lost wallet. (They didn't find it. The police phoned two days later to say it had been recovered, but by then her husband had cancelled all his credit and other cards.) Bearing in mind the fees involved, Paul, Shayla, and Penny eventually decided to send slightly random and unpredictable amounts, something like $125 to $250 US, every two to three months.

As Paul reported the outcome of the meeting to Yvonne, he noted it was hard to know the cost of living in small town Lebanon. "The info on the web seems to be geared more towards Westerners wanting to live a European lifestyle in Beirut. There it looks like a bundle of everyday goods and services costs about forty percent less than we pay here. The stipends would therefore be minimal but should help significantly with the extra food and clothing costs our family's relatives are facing while housing our family."

Karl Golds took the next run at strengthening communications. "Greetings friends!" he wrote. "Just checking in. Looking at the notes below, I regret to acknowledge that we, at least the Americans, did not manage to send a CARE package for Christmas. Perhaps we can focus our energies in the New Year. Do we have a mailing address or other way of sending physical items?" He mentioned that he was constantly mindful of the Mousa family living in poor conditions "while we enjoy riches and comfort. Any news from our Canadian partners? You are in our thoughts and prayers too."

Several days later, Paul groaned. A little groan and not very long, but one reflecting his mild disappointment that nobody from All Saints had yet responded to Karl. He didn't mind composing another email but feared the all too familiar pattern was again emerging: many people at All Saints seeing something as important, committing the congregation, cheering from the sidelines, but leaving it to just one or two people to organize and realize the project. Nevertheless, there was an opportunity to propose another visit in conjunction with an upcoming concert.

A local jazz band had proposed the church sell refreshments as a refugee fundraiser at its Mardi Gras concert to be held at All Saints. The amount of money raised would likely be small, but it would be good publicity. "Anybody from Seattle who wants to be part of this would be welcome," Paul wrote. "I know it's tough for those working to get here on time on a Friday night, but we'd be glad to give you a place to stay." He closed by mentioning a recent article in the Vancouver newspaper that said the influx of Syrian refugees had created a backlog in English classes. "I'm hoping the silver lining in the black cloud of the current slowdown in new arrivals is that the language waitlists will become shorter."

Yvonne and Paul continued their email exchange in the following days. "I am so upset with the US political scene," Yvonne wrote, "with these latest restrictive rules about refugee matters, among other things, but all the more glad for this opportunity to work with you guys."

Paul considered this comment and wondered if he should respond. He normally preferred to stay out of his neighbours' internal affairs, but the latest developments specifically concerned Syrian refugees. President Trump's executive order on his fifth day in office not only barred citizens of seven Muslim-majority countries from entering the United States for ninety days—"protecting the nation from radical Islamic terrorists" while new vetting processes were supposedly being developed—they totally banned the entry of all refugees from Syria. In addition, America's refugee program would be suspended for four months, and Barrack Obama's cap of admitting 110,000 refugees annually would be reduced to 50,000. Priority would be given to refugees who had experienced religious persecution, which seemed to be code language for giving priority to Christians.

Fifty thousand a year, thought Paul. *For a nation the size of the United States, that's almost saying there is no refugee program.* The Canadian government's website showed Canada, with one-tenth the population of the United States, had admitted 39,700 refugees from Syria alone in the fourteen months since November 2015. Of these, 14,000 had been privately sponsored. An additional 18,000 applications from Syrians, half currently in Lebanon, were still being processed.

How could two such culturally similar countries hold such diametrically opposed views about Syrians? *The same way America erroneously convinced itself about weapons of mass destruction in Iraq*, Paul thought. *I didn't get how that happened, either.* He decided that he needed to send some sort of message of support to Yvonne.

"Hang in there," he wrote to Yvonne. "The fundamental decency of America will eventually prevail. We also experience ripple effects on this side of the border. They're not as profound as what you're facing, but it's hard for me to imagine that the overall impact will be positive. I think there's now a higher level of interest and investment here in American politics, and a greater desire to see healing in your civic culture, than at any time since the turmoil of the sixties."

Paul's forebodings proved all too prescient. Just one day after his message to Yvonne, a twenty-seven-year-old white Canadian with a taste for far-right social media entered a mosque in Quebec City and fatally shot six males. Prime Minister Trudeau quickly condemned what he described as a terrorist attack on Muslims, a community that he emphasized was an important part of Canada's national fabric.

But life had to go on. Paul made his way to the Western Union office to wire money to Lebanon. His concern mounted when the funds had not been picked up after several days, but it turned out to be a simple communication gap: the Lebanese office either hadn't alerted the family about the transfer or the family had missed the message. All was well and the family was extremely grateful.

When Paul sat at his computer to update everyone about the latest developments, he realized he wanted to say a great deal. Mostly he wanted to describe a memorial service at a mosque for the Quebec shooting victims, but he decided to insert that story between information more directly related to the refugee sponsorship. *I hope all this really is of interest to everybody and not only me,* he thought. *Surely, they'll want to know about the premier of the province and local mayors attending the service.*

February 8, 2017
Paul to SRAG and the welcoming team:

> Just before I wired some more money to Lebanon, a senior gave me a contribution somewhat apologetically because she felt it was quite small. I told her the amount was perfect because it would cover the fees and enable your entire donation to go to the family. She felt good about this, her sense of inadequacy dispelled.

> A bureaucratic inanity is that, although Western Union can only wire US dollars, not Canadian dollars, to Lebanon, it can receive funds from me here in Canada only in Canadian currency, not US dollars.

> When I arrived home from wiring the money last Friday morning, a message from the Iraqi family we sponsored a few years ago—who you met at our joint dinner last August— invited our congregation to midday prayers at their mosque for the six Muslim victims in the shooting in Quebec City on January 29. The number of non-Muslim guests at the mosque was modest, but they included a handful of politicians who spoke well at the end of the service.

The first to speak was the premier of British Columbia who, uncharacteristically, avoided turning the event into a photo op—all the more remarkable because she faces the electorate in May. One of the two mayors said he wished the sermon had been taped because he felt it would be entirely appropriate to incorporate into his church service on Sunday—a thought that had also run through my mind, despite the exhortation to remain steadfast in the Islamic faith.

The theme across both Muslim and Christian speakers was a call for something more than tolerance, namely an active embracing of diversity "within a single human community." Rather than assigning blame or dwelling on losses, the priority seemed to be on using this tragedy to spark conversations across religious and cultural boundaries, stepping out of comfort zones to build friendships. In many ways, I'm finding that our refugee sponsorship partnership is helping me— pushing me—to do just that.

So in the spirit of friendship, let me reiterate that All Saints would be glad to host anybody who wants to be part of a bake sale fundraiser (but mainly publicity about refugees) at the Creole Jazz Band concert for Mardi Gras at our church. It's not so much that we need help as it would be nice to continue strengthening our relationships.

Postscript about prayers at the mosque:
February 3: All Saints church office to the congregation:

Good morning All Saints family and friends,

Today at 12:30 p.m., there will be a Prayer for the Dead held at the Masjid Al Mubtadi and Islamic Cultural Centre. We are all invited to attend.

Here are a few things to be aware of if you are able to attend:

- Usually when entering the mosque, you would wash your hands, face, and feet, so you may be asked to do so.

- Covering your arms and feet (i.e., long sleeves) is encouraged and, women, wear a simple head scarf if you are comfortable doing so.

All are welcome.

Because of the special nature of the prayer service and the invitation to everyone in the community, chairs were set up for guests in the opening that connected the men's worship space with the centre's gymnasium. This seating meant that guests did not have to be segregated by sex, remove shoes, or kneel on the carpet. They were not asked to participate in the ritual washing in another area of the building. The two female politicians who spoke at the end of the service wore headscarves, but women guests who remained outside the worship space did not. Most stayed for refreshments and mingled afterwards.

All That Jazz

Plans for the refreshment sale at the February 17 jazz concert were slowly gelling. Penny jumped right in. "I'll definitely be at the concert, and I'll invite as many friends as I can. I can help with set-up, greeting, and clean up. I'm looking forward to it!"

Justine, on the other hand, sent her regrets from Seattle. "I wish our family could join you, but we are departing the following day for a few days of mid-winter school break in Northern Washington."

Shayla made a brief request for baking donations during the Sunday morning announcement time. She also contacted a youth leader to see if any teens would staff the table at the concert. *It's a nice way of involving them,* she thought, *with a fun local band that had connections to the congregation.*

With the organizing well started, Shayla decided it was time for a break from preparing an information poster about Syrian refugees for the concert. Sprawled on her two-toned couch with the local newspaper, one leg dangling and the other resting on a throw pillow, she silently cheered when she encountered a substantial article about the forthcoming concert, complete with a photo of the five band members. Her mouth drooped as she realized the journalist didn't have all the details correct. After a moment's thought, she sprang to the notebook computer in the dining room and composed a note to Paul.

"I just read the concert announcement in the news rag. I couldn't help but be a little concerned that important details were reported in error." The article claimed the refugee family had already arrived and that all the proceeds, rather than just those from refreshment sales, would go towards the family. "What do you think we should do to inform the ticket-purchasing public before or on the night of the concert about the misunderstanding? I want to run this by you before talking with the band leader."

Paul checked his email a half hour after Shayla sent her message. *Those are nice errors*, he thought, *that might give attendance a boost. Too bad we need to be ethical and not mislead the public.* He wondered if there was a way of making a correction that wouldn't involve a lot of effort and drama. He considered the options for almost two hours before sitting down to respond to Shayla.

"I didn't quite go dumpster diving," he wrote, "but I did have to rummage through the recycling bin to find the offending article. My inclination is to downplay the errors and simply ask the band to clarify in a low-key manner during the concert that things are not entirely as reported in the paper (but thank the newspaper for the publicity and getting it mostly right)." He explained that it struck him as too late to make corrections for the general public and that the errors were within the norm for local newspapers. "They run on a shoestring and the paragraph describing Mardi Gras bears an uncanny resemblance to the Wikipedia article on Mardi Gras. I view local reporters as busy, underpaid, and generally doing a decent job with what is sometimes ambiguous source information."

Late in the afternoon on the day of the concert, the Palmer family from Seattle tersely emailed that they were trapped in traffic on the I-5 freeway near Everett. They were uncertain how much of the concert they would miss. When they eventually dashed through the doors of All Saints, intermission had just begun. Judi steered them away from the refreshment table—the bake sale was well in hand—and instead introduced them to Natalie and Rona. "Our two friends from Syria and Iraq, who are helping us make contact with the Mousa family."

The Palmers sent a note of thanks a week later. They said they had been honoured to be part of the Dixieland event and enjoyed talking with the two Middle Eastern women advocating for the Mousas. "It's so heartening for us to continue to be some small part of extending welcome, especially as our country's leadership is not stepping up, to say the very least. And thanks for listening to our theories on that. Obviously, we in the US have a lot of work to do. A special thanks for the very warm welcome, hosting, and feasting. It was a joy."

Catching Up

"Fret" was too strong a word, yet Vicki was increasingly aware that the welcoming team had not met as a full group for a couple of months. Members had certainly emailed each other and engaged in many one-on-one conversations, but these interactions were task oriented and didn't provide much opportunity to explore less urgent or more general matters.

"Why don't you come over to my house," she invited the team, "and just chat about what's happened over the past little while? We need to keep plugging away at forging a strong team that won't crumble when the stresses build after the family arrives."

The evening of February 23 worked for everyone, at least initially. Just before the supper hour, Penny texted Vicki. "I might not be able to make it tonight. I have an employee with car trouble and we're still waiting for the tow truck. If the tow doesn't show, then I'll have to drive her home. Please don't wait for me. I'll come whenever I can make it."

The other three arrived at Vicki's home within a few minutes of each other. Paul filled his napkin with a piece of banana loaf, a cluster of green grapes, and three slices of Gouda cheese stacked beside some water crackers. "I'm going to stop eating dinner on the evenings you host us, Vicki," he said. "You look after us so well."

"I'll say what I always do," Vicki said, smiling in acknowledgement. "I like hosting and I enjoy having you people over."

"I'm glad you brought us together again," Paul said as he settled into the upholstered armchair. "I was thinking along those lines when I received an unexpected prod from an email that included an aside about refugee sponsorship. My correspondent's comments were sobering and reinforce the importance of building a strong team." He unfolded a single sheet of paper and read the text he had highlighted in yellow:

> I've been on the periphery of a sponsorship group for a year now. My cousin, together with her closest friend of twenty years, formed a sponsorship group with several others late 2015. The family of six arrived from Syria last April or May, so the formal sponsorship will be coming to an end in the next few months.
>
> I have watched and listened to the process with great interest, and not a little horror, as decisions, not always good, were made and group dynamics threatened to run good intentions off the rails. I began to think early on that, one day, perhaps many years down the road, some very smart person will write a book

analyzing the good and the bad about what Canada has done and how it's been done.

So when I think of your situation in light of what I've been watching from the sidelines, I'm struck by how far you have yet to go. And I can say with some confidence, you have no idea what's coming!

"I don't think I'm naïve," Judi said with a furrowed brow, "but that sounds excessive to me."

"Maybe. Maybe not," Shayla added. "Every once in a while, I wonder if some of our folk are a little naïve. Some are so happy with all that's happening in this project. They don't feel the same concerns as us. They don't have the Neufeld's voices in the back of their mind about the ups and downs of All Saints' previous sponsorship experience."

Judi didn't think the previous speakers meant to disparage anybody but felt uneasy with the tenor of the comments. "It's been good that we've had the Seattle connection while we're waiting," she said, trying to direct the conversation onto a more positive track, "because that's forced us to work together as a group and get used to doing things together." She watched Paul's unsuccessful attempt to stack his cheese gracefully on a cracker. "I wholeheartedly agree that it's going to be so important for us to have good communication and ensure we all know what each other is doing. We have to be intentional about working well together."

A smile slowly crossed Vicki's face. "I hadn't thought about SRAG's effect on All Saints, but you know, one of their contributions might be that they'll help keep our local people on their best behaviour. We won't want to look bad in front of our visitors, especially when they're the ones who've made all this possible."

Judi nodded in agreement. "You're probably right. I don't know how much good Mount Olivet will end up doing on the world scene, but they're certainly adding to our lives. And stretching us, too. In good ways."

"Here's something cool that's just happened because of SRAG's caring," Shayla said. "Yes, it's small scale, but it's significant." She scanned the group to ensure she had everyone's attention. "My neighbours are atheists, but they think that supporting refugees should be more than just something done within a religion. So they've given us $100. Atheists donating to a church! How's that for bridge building as a result of this project?"

"So what does that bring our total to in our Lebanon fund?" Vicki asked.

"We made about $430 at the jazz concert," Judi said, "and another $40 selling leftovers at church the following Sunday. So that's $470."

"The second cheque from Seattle is roughly $250 in Canadian dollars," Paul said. "And now this $100. The total must be a little over $800. Not bad, considering we didn't really set out to do any of this. Things just happened."

Penny finally arrived, letting herself in the unlocked front door and climbing the stairs to the second floor living room. Having unobtrusively taken the first seat available, she now joined the conversation. "I heard you saying something about being stretched and learning when I came in. I'm really having my horizons broadened and simplistic stereotypes challenged this year.

"One of our employees wasn't feeling well a week or two ago and because he normally takes transit, I drove him home. This was the first time I'd talked with him about his personal life.

"He came from Syria with his parents, brother, and sister eight months ago. They left Syria in 2007 and were living in Dubai. He still has three brothers in Syria. I just can't imagine! He told me it only took two months to get to Canada. I told him he was very lucky.

"I think he is still in shock as to what has happened to his country. He said it would be like Canada having a war. He said Syria was just like Canada, with different groups living together side by side. But he does love Canada and is very happy to be here. We now have five employees who were originally from Syria, all because Canada opened its doors."

"And all that most of us knew about Syria a few years ago was that the capital is Damascus," Paul said. "Getting back to practical matters, how much of this $800 should we send in our next installment to Lebanon? And when? I was thinking towards the end of March, before Easter."

With more money available than anticipated, Judi suggested half of the $800.

"I wonder, if we up the ante, do we create a bigger change in their circumstances?" Shayla asked. Vicki liked the idea of smaller amounts sent more frequently, but varying the amount each time.

"You'd think we'd have this all figured out by now," Paul said, "but it's hard when we don't know how much money we'll have available and when we don't have all the information about our family's situation. Even then, it might not be clear. We've all heard stories of well-intentioned people throwing money at problems and ending up doing more harm than good.

"I went to a world development and missions exhibition a few weeks ago," he continued, "where I met a representative from a Christian aid organization that works in Lebanon. They provide humanitarian aid to refugees who have made their way into that country. They don't proselytize, but when recipients ask, 'Why are you doing this?' they reply, 'Because we're Christians.' That opens up a conversation that might last three minutes, three weeks, or three months. They chose to work in Lebanon because it's one of the few countries in the Middle East where religion can be freely discussed.

"This guy knew a lot about refugees in Lebanon, so I tried pumping him for what he thought would be an appropriate amount of aid for us to provide. He wouldn't name a figure. All he said was that his organization gives the same amount to everyone, which I presume is to avoid having to judge endless claims and deal with complaints of unfairness.

"He then commented, 'We don't want to foster dependency. There are ways...there are ways for people to support themselves over there.' Whether he was referring to the underground economy, networks of family relationships, or what was going on, I don't know. In any event, I was surprised that he didn't encourage me to send more money to our family."

"You know," Shayla said, "the UN website suggests that by giving cash rather than, say, food, parents are less likely to pull their kids out of school to go to work. They are less likely to be exploited, such as being forced to send girls out for prostitution. It can get really desperate.

"The money we send to our family isn't intended to fully support them. We're just helping out, a gesture of goodwill, keeping their hopes up."

"I think more money will come in once we've exhausted this $800," Vicki said. "So perhaps pay more each time?"

Shayla said, "I know they're incredibly grateful. They're praying for us and hope to see us soon. I think we're dealing with mature people who happen to be in a tough situation. We don't have to become their nanny."

With consensus seemingly a far way off, Paul made a proposal. "Why don't I wire $300 or so at the end of March?" Then he promptly changed the topic. "I have a few other things to contribute to our show-and-tell session. Did everybody see that Tima Kurdi is writing a book about her experience as a Syrian who came to Canada? And of course, about her nephew."

Heads nodded. They had all read the article in the local newspaper. Judi turned to Shayla. "Tell me about your meeting with our member of Parliament."

Shayla looked blank for a moment and then perked up. "He said that as an MP, he can't really do much to hurry the process along.

He had me fill out a form with our family's UN tracking number. He can try to hand it to whoever and make enquiries for certain cases. But our family isn't in crisis, so he can't run interference. Pastor Ellen was there with me. The bottom line is that our family just needs to make it through the system. There are thousands of cases."

"But some refugees get here quickly," Judi countered. She leaned forward on the couch. "My co-worker's church got two families already."

"They were likely part of the 25,000 thrust," Shayla speculated. "The reason the 25,000 went so quickly was that they were simply clearing the backlog. Under the previous Harper government, the processing of claims was extremely slow. Trudeau's new government hired a lot of temporary paper-pushers to expedite those files. Many of those old cases already had been cleared and were pretty much ready to come to Canada. It wasn't new stuff. It was people already in the system who were waiting.

"Now that the backlog is cleared and the 25,000 target's been met, the feds have scaled back their staff. New types of backlog seem to have emerged in Canada where English classes are full and housing hard to find."

A siren wailed faintly in the distance. *Probably an ambulance,* Paul thought. "The other update I'm interested in," he said, "is how things went at the jazz concert."

"Natalie came," Shayla said. "Rona too. Rona was dressed in black because a relative had passed away from a heart attack. Many refugees struggle with health concerns brought on by trauma and extreme stress. There's a lot of heart attacks and strokes."

"They arrive in North America in bad shape and life is still tough when they get here," Penny elaborated.

"I think Natalie and her circle are very grateful for what we're doing," Shayla said, stroking her chin in thought. "They think it's a Christian duty to look after persecuted Christians, so they're taken aback that I'm not worried about what religion people are.

They seem to think Canada is not letting in enough Christians. In their view, Muslims can apply to other countries because they have more options."

"Rona said her family waited for five years to come to Canada. They had initially applied to the United States, but only some of her family were accepted. So they said no and waited another two years for Canada to accept all of them."

A few eyebrows rose at this news. How difficult it must be to turn down safety for yourself in order to keep the family together. And then to wait in exile for a couple more years.

"I bought concert tickets for the Badawi family, who didn't show. Partha is struggling. His hand is painful, but he has to carry heavy loads in his delivery work. The guy beside him in the truck smokes pot continually. Partha was feeling so ill." Shayla shook her head.

"Going back to whether Canada should give priority to Christians," Penny said, joining in, "Pastor Ellen made an interesting comment. Judi and I were telling her how things went at the concert—she didn't attend because a family member is dying—and the conversation turned to my son's German girlfriend, who is bitterly against Syrian refugees. She gets that attitude from her parents. I can understand why they might develop it, with Germany having been flooded with about a million refugees. In any event, Pastor said that when people use 'them' and 'us' language, it often means they've never developed a relationship with any of 'them'. When you know people personally, you're less likely to lump them together in the same one-dimensional category."

Vicki nodded her head in strong agreement. "Tamas and his family came to the board game session at the church last Saturday afternoon. That's one of the ways we get different people to rub shoulders. He and I got talking about the Koran and the Bible, comparing how each came together as books and the nature of holy inspiration."

"I didn't win any games, that evening," Shayla contributed, "but I too had some good conversations. I asked about music and got two different takes on how it's seen in Islam. The Badawi family has music in their house. In Tamas' house, on the other hand, there is zero music. They don't listen to music. Their kids are excused from school music lessons. They view music as something that will fill your head and then your head won't have enough space for memorizing the Koran. The Koran is to be memorized over your lifetime. Music is not seen as having any value."

"So Islam must be like Christianity," Paul concluded. "There's a range of beliefs. Some Christians believe that the only singing should be Psalms or that there should be no musical accompaniment. I think a few sects don't have any music at all in their gatherings."

"But one of the differences in Middle Eastern culture compared to here," Judi said, "is that religion has a stronger, more central role, infusing all the decisions they make. Zrebar is studying hard. I'm not sure if she was joking, but she said she's working up to daring to wear the *niqab*. I just said, 'Don't.'"

"For us, religion is often a little add-on," Penny observed. "I've seen that Middle Eastern approach in a few places in East Asia, where I sensed religion permeates everything. Going back a few generations to my own ancestors, religion was probably much more central in their lives, too."

A few heads turned towards Vicki as she stretched in her seat. "Wow," she said, "time is passing. We had a lot to catch up on." Suddenly aware of the implication of what she said, she quickly added, "You're welcome to stay as long as you want. If you've more to share, I'd love to hear it."

"You already know that I have lots of contact with Leandra in Lebanon and try to treat it like a lifeline among friends," Shayla said. "They send me pictures to show me something of their lives.

"I had this long text conversation with Leandra and couldn't figure out how she did it. How was she texting me in English when she doesn't know the language? Google Translate? Apparently she would phone Natalie here in Canada and ask for the necessary vocabulary so she could respond. Natalie would translate, using this opportunity to encourage the entire Mousa family to work hard on learning some English." Shayla smiled. "Just because people are in tough situations doesn't mean they can't be resourceful."

"Speaking of phones," Paul interjected, "I met a young engineer a few days ago who had volunteered in Iraq. He said that, in Iraq, because a particular phone plan might be good for local calling but a different one better for international calling, people have multiple plans with multiple phone numbers because they're dirt cheap. They use whatever number allows for the cheapest calling. However, that means multiple SIM cards, so you can buy phones in the Middle East that hold more than one SIM card. You can't get those phones in North America."

"What's a SIM card?" Vicki asked.

"It's like a chip in your phone," Judi replied. "If you only call in Canada and roam occasionally in the States, there's no reason to change a card or even know they exist. When I travel internationally, I usually buy a cheap plan at the airport where I land. They put a new chip in my phone to connect with local networks and I get a temporary new phone number. Then I replace it with my Canadian card when I come home."

"Oh, okay," Vicki said. "I know about those. I just didn't know what they were called."

"My last contribution to show and tell," Penny said, "is a poll revealing that one-quarter of Canadians agree with Trump about immigration. I'm the first to admit there are issues with bringing in a lot of newcomers, but at the same time, the intermingling brings a lot of people together. I think something beautiful is happening between the Seattle people and us, and between Natalie, Rona, and our congregation."

Vicki agreed, adding, "I'm not convinced that we're solving very many of the world's immediate problems by what we're doing for one refugee family, but we're certainly changing us."

"I would never have been to a service in the mosque if a refugee family hadn't invited us to go," Paul said.

"Yes," Judi agreed. "We all touch each other's lives. Natalie and Rona met the American family who came up for the concert."

"And because we're helping refugees," Vicki concluded, "the word goes back to Iraq and Syria about what life is really like in North America. This helps break down some of their misconceptions and stereotypes of us. We're not all godless and focused exclusively on money. This is how bad attitudes and incorrect stereotypes around the world get chipped away. We start seeing one another as real, complicated people. We have differences, but we also have similarities. We learn how to become comfortable with each other."

WAITING CALMLY
WITH OCCASIONAL
JITTERS

Health Scare

Justine in Seattle was looking for help assembling a photo album. She prefaced her request with some political commentary. "We were so sorry to hear of the mosque shooting in Quebec," she wrote, "and sad, too, that it received so little attention from our administration. The politics in our country are circus-like and many of us are trying to find a constructive, hope-filled path forward. The recent court ruling on the immigration ban was something to cheer about, but who knows what the future holds." Then she asked for photos of church gatherings and families, and a sentence or two of greeting that could be sent to the Mousas.

Shayla had a few thoughts to share about the photo album, hoping it would be digital because parcels were prohibitively expensive, but mostly this seemed a good time to ensure everyone was up to date. She explained that she'd been texting frequently. "The children are healthy and growing. Life in Lebanon is really expensive, but they can't work and therefore have no income. They need about $500 US per month for living expenses, outside of housing because they're able to live rent-free with their sister." Leandra was shocked to learn about the cost of living in Canada, but Shayla considered it important to inform her about local conditions.

Shayla, more than anyone at All Saints, eagerly awaited the Mousa family's safe arrival on Canadian soil. She heard the whoosh of an incoming text message as she closed the car door with her hip, her shoulder bag swaying while she clasped two work binders to her chest. An hour and a half passed before she had the opportunity to read her personal messages. One was good news from Leandra: Canadian officials in Beirut were now processing the Mousas' refugee application, starting with a medical examination.

How long would it take to receive all the results of this screening for contagious diseases? Nobody on the welcoming team knew, but they assumed it would take much longer than they thought it should. Four weeks passed with no news.

Paul awoke early, to his chagrin, and made himself a cup of coffee. He returned to his bedroom and placed the mug on the nightstand. Propping two pillows against the teak headboard, he slipped back under the covers and began casually flipping through the new emails on his tablet. He sat upright as he read Shayla's email. "Just got email from the Mousa family with some pictures. Yamo on a stretcher with a dripline (?). And either Leandra or her sister is in the hospital. We are meant to pray for them."

Paul was on full alert, wondering if the medical screening had found something wrong and whether the family now risked being rejected by the Canadian government. "Calm down," he ordered himself. "Wait for more information and don't jump to conclusions. Shayla probably received only a few words of fractured English in the text with the photos." He decided his best strategy would simply be to trust that things would eventually work out. "More of the same," he lamented. "Incomplete and ambiguous information that keeps us off balance."

Even after hearing more from Lebanon, Shayla still couldn't understand the photo of Yamo on the stretcher. After a while, it became clear that it was his sister-in-law who was the patient. Although poor news, the sister-in-law was at least a legal resident of Lebanon and therefore probably entitled to the same medical care as her citizen husband. Her Syrian relatives, the Mousa family, had no rights whatsoever.

Abandoning her attempt to further decipher the latest Lebanese communication, Shayla checked for other messages. Her face brightened as she saw an email from the office of her member of Parliament. *I assumed we were just getting the polite brush-off at that meeting a few weeks ago*, she thought, *yet here they are following up.* Perhaps the outlook was not entirely bleak.

March 31, 2017
Parliamentary constituency assistant to Shayla:

> Good afternoon Ms. Dunbar,
>
> I hope this message finds you well. I followed up regarding the Mousa family, and I wanted to send you a quick message to update you. I learned that the criminality verifications have been completed and passed. The medical examinations, which were scheduled for March 2, were completed and passed, which is good news.
>
> The eligibility and security verifications are forthcoming. I was advised to follow up again in 6–8 weeks to check the status of the application. I hope you find this information helpful; if you have any questions please feel free to contact me here at the office. Thank you, and enjoy your weekend!

Judi happened to be chatting with Pastor Ellen the next day and passed this news along to her. "I know that assistant," Ellen said. "She's great."

"I wonder," Judi continued, "if this timeline means that it's possible that all the screening will be done in eight weeks and that transportation approval could come soon after? We'd better alert everyone to this possibility so they can watch for furniture and accommodation leads." The family's arrival was shifting from an abstract concept to a more concrete reality, one that might soon entail some actual work and attention to schedules.

Paul mused along these lines as he rested at his kitchen table, ruefully noting the possibility that serious house hunting might start just as he was leaving for a month's vacation. *Big help, I'll be,* he thought.

The next morning, half a dozen people lined up at the payday loan office. They seemed like regulars because they knew exactly what to do. Paul's turn at the wicket to wire money came after only fifteen minutes. *I wonder what people would think,* he asked himself, *if they knew I enjoy my visits to the loans office? It's bright and clean, and behind the security glass, the clerk is pleasant and efficient. Actually, so are the clients.* The clientele seemed mainly young and male, but otherwise didn't fit Paul's stereotypes of who might visit such an office. *If anybody sees me here, they'll probably wonder what kind of financial trouble I'm in. I've probably heated up the gossip network just by coming in.*

Paul and Shayla exchanged notes the next day to confirm that the money had transferred successfully. "Yup," Shayla wrote. "The Mousas just sent me a picture of the receipt. All good then!"

Road to Emmaus

The Gospel reading for the third Sunday after Easter was Luke's account of two disciples walking on the road to Emmaus shortly after the crucifixion of Jesus. A stranger joined them and asked about their conversation. They explained that Jesus, "a prophet mighty in deed and word," had been killed and that some women at his tomb had reported a vision of angels, who said Jesus was alive again. Jerusalem was abuzz with this story.

The All Saints worship leader—Pastor Ellen was away on Synod business—recapped the story as he began the sermon. "Two disciples were coming away from the intensity of the past few days. They felt that the path they had started following, Jesus' way, had come to a dead end. They couldn't make sense of their experiences; it seemed so pointless. They needed to get back to how things had been before. Yet something unexpected and someone unrecognized turned this situation on its head. A stranger approached them and they eventually realized it was their risen Lord.

"I want to pick out three things from this story and invite you to reflect on them. First, this story wouldn't be a story if these two disciples hadn't welcomed the stranger into their conversation and then later into their home. Do you think people in our area are open to welcoming the stranger?"

A slight rustle rippled through the congregation. It was much nicer to sit passively and receive words of encouragement than to examine one's life. And what exactly was meant by strangers, welcoming them, and our area? The mood was a little more attentive, perhaps even wary, as the sermon continued.

"Secondly, the stranger helps them to make sense of something in their lives. How many of you, in talking with a stranger have come to better understand your own life? What is it about a stranger that allows us to see our lives more clearly?"

Drat. These were good questions, not easily sloughed off as irrelevant preacher talk.

"And then, thirdly, after Christ vanished from their sight, they went and told their fellow disciples about their encounter with the risen Lord. Do you tell others about your 'God encounters' and meaningful spiritual moments? Why or why not?

"I want to invite you to take a few minutes right now and talk with a few people around you about one or two of those questions."

Oh, no, not another one of those touchy-feely exercises where you have to "share" intimate details with your neighbour. Heavens, some of the people near me are complete strangers. What can I say to them?
Oh.
Strangers. Guess that's the point of the exercise.

"This discussion would probably work best in groups of three or four, especially if there's a stranger in your midst. And I'm not going to put anybody on the spot by asking you to report out afterwards. These are weighty questions, and our discussion today is just intended to kick-start your personal reflections over the coming days.

"Feel free to move around as you break into groups now. And look around to ensure nobody's left out. Somebody may choose not to speak, and that's fine, but everybody should have the opportunity to listen."

Not many people moved at first, but gradually groups formed and the noise level rose. A few individuals were obviously not participating, but only one looked distinctly uncomfortable as he studied his hymn book. Several managed to avoid the questions by describing who lived in their neighbourhood or talking about times they had moved to a strange, new place. Most, though, seemed at least partly engaged with the questions.

After several minutes, the leader brought the exercise to a close. "Early in our Bible reading, one of the verses said, 'While they were talking and discussing together, Jesus himself drew near and went with them, but their eyes were kept from recognizing him.' I wonder if that might have happened again just now? In any event, it's time to bring our discussions to a close and return to a more ordered and predictable form of worship."

Over coffee after the service, opinion was divided as to whether the sermon had been designed to get the congregation thinking about the role of refugees and immigrants in Canadian society or whether it just happened to be compatible with this topic. "Speaking of which," Shayla said, "I've received a text from Leandra saying that her family is finding it tough with five people living in one room for so many months. They're wondering if there's any way of speeding up the process."

"Probably not," Bruce replied as he placed an empty mug on a table. "At least, not if the recent CBC reports are to be believed. Our government seems to be slowing down, not speeding up. Once the feds met their commitment of 25,000 Syrian refugees, they wound down the temporary staff in their processing system. Something like 500 employees dropped to 70 now working in the Middle East. There's almost 200 sponsorship groups who've been waiting for more than a year for their Syrians to arrive. It seems like having met its election promise, the government doesn't care anymore. I know humanitarian issues can be complicated, but this feels cynical to me.

"Another tidbit I picked up," he added, "is that more than one million Syrian refugees are currently living in Lebanon. That's the highest number of refugees per capita in the world. Lebanon only has about seven million people and isn't the most stable of countries."

One of the ushers drifted into the conversation. "The regular, permanent staff in the government is being stretched even thinner as they deal with the increasing number of asylum seekers fleeing Donald Trump's America and crossing into Canada. Nice of the States to export their problems to us." He paused. "I take that back. That was a cheap and unfair dig. There's more to it than that."

Bruce nodded in agreement. "There's always more to news stories, I think. Still, the fact remains that two dozen asylum seekers from the United States were picked up in a snowy field along the Manitoba border on a single day in February. The temperatures were subzero, so they must have been pretty desperate to try slipping into Canada that way in such weather. And this wasn't an isolated case."

The audience murmured its assent. They too had heard the reports of asylum seekers along the American border in Manitoba and Quebec.

Political Advocacy

The visiting preacher came from a Vancouver church that had given a former civilian translator in the KGB six years of sanctuary in its basement. Many at All Saints were familiar with the sad story. Sergei had arrived in British Columbia in 1997 on a student visa to pursue graduate studies in Russian–Japanese cultural relations. Despite having been forthright about his background, the federal government ultimately deemed him too great a security risk to grant him permanent residency in Canada. It ordered him deported back to Russia in 2009, at which point the church's support of Sergei took a distinctly practical turn when he turned to it for help. In a bewildering move, the government conferred Canadian citizenship on his Russian-born wife and son, but did not repeal Sergei's deportation order. A weary Sergei finally complied with the order in 2015, leaving his family behind in Canada and saying goodbye to his city of eighteen years.

This Sunday therefore struck Paul as an especially appropriate time to update the All Saints congregation on the status of the Mousa family. Standing with one hand on the lectern at announcement time, he mentioned that with another cash installment having been sent to Lebanon, the kitty was now down to $50. "If anybody cares to help replenish it, that would be great.

"On another note, one of the welcoming team heard of a refugee support group that organized some temporary housing through the bailiff as part of bankruptcy proceedings. That doesn't sound very appealing and yet we have to be practical, so we're going to follow up and see what this entailed and how it's working out.

"The main thing I want to tell you, though, is about a letter Shayla sent to our local member of Parliament in Ottawa. I'll read it to you in its entirety. It's dated May 26." The letter began by reminding Andrew that she and Pastor Ellen had previously met with him about a refugee family. She related the many negative effects of living in overcrowded limbo that the family had experienced:

fatigue, high blood pressure, minimal schooling for the children, and so on. "They are losing faith in the willingness of the Canadian government to process their application and allow them into our country. We, too, are wondering why it is taking so long and hope than you and your wonderful staff may be able to look into the Mousa family's application once again."

The couple of weeks it took for Shayla to receive a reply seemed like months to her. When it did arrive, the news was poor. It seemed that nothing had happened since early March and that progress over the next half a year was likely to be almost as slow. The constituency assistant had written: "Two of the four criteria for acceptance have been passed and two more are in the works. We can therefore expect to wait at least another five to seven months."

Shayla passed this news along to All Saints and Mount Olivet, ending her email with "Stay strong and stay connected." Her message generated some discussion about gathering more money to send to Lebanon now that it seemed likely the Mousas would remain in the Middle East for the rest of 2017. Among the practical details and exasperation about the prolonged process, the thread of gratitude and hope remained vibrant.

Lori-Ann in Seattle agreed that the process was slow. "But I continue to be so grateful to All Saints and Canada for extending this welcome that will eventually bring a family to safety and a new future." She said her church prayed for the family every Sunday and their pictures were in the Sunday school room for the children to see. "We showed the kids, using a world map, where the Mousas lived and now live, and where they will travel when it's time. We send encouragement; there is hope!"

Just one week after the discouraging news that more long waits were probable, the Mousas asked for the address of their sponsors for an interview late in June. Neither Shayla nor the family was clear exactly who was the official sponsor: the person who signed the papers, All Saints as the host church, or the Canadian Lutheran

World Relief. An "excited and scared" Shayla hastily sent a note to the welcoming team asking for clarification so that she could pass it along to Lebanon.

Pastor Ellen promptly replied, "All Saints is the sponsor and CLWR is the Canadian government sponsorship agreement holder. So give them All Saints' contact information." She also passed along some generic information from a workshop she'd attended about the interview process:

- At the interview, they ask the refugee applicant questions to ensure accuracy and credibility, and then the officer determines if they are eligible for resettlement.
- If approved, the refugee applicant must get police background checks from every country in which they have ever resided.
- The visa office also does a thorough background security check using the assistance of the Canadian Security Intelligence Service (known as CSIS). If there is anything suspicious in the file, it is scrupulously reviewed and investigations are conducted.
- A refugee applicant can be barred from entering Canada on the basis of security, serious criminality, organized criminality or human rights violations.

Joanna confirmed that as All Saints' signatory, Shayla could also pass along Joanna's contact information. The refugee approval process might be glacial, but at least it had not stalled. Had the latest enquiry to the member of Parliament helped things move a little faster? The group would never know, but they figured it probably hadn't hurt.

Still Waiting

Spirits sagged as the summer passed with no further developments. Even nature seemed cranky, with wildfires in the province's interior forcing thousands to evacuate and hurricanes pummelling the southern United States.

Karl in Seattle somehow sensed that the All Saints group needed a boost. "I hope all of you are well. Just checking in. How are we doing in terms of monthly support? Shall we take up another collection?" He added a postscript. "Many thanks to Canada for sharing your forest fire smoke with us. We've really enjoyed it this summer." A grinning emoji ended the email.

Shayla promptly replied to say that her family had relished slipping across the border in early August to visit the alpine meadows of Mount Baker, the most northern in the chain of volcanoes stretching from California to Washington. "The air was great and the hiking gorgeous!" She mentioned that the last money had been wired from Canada two weeks before and that, although Canada had been busy with Haitian folk crossing into Quebec and the Rainbow Railroad of gay Chechen men, the overall refugee acceptance process was very slow. "I'm acutely aware that Pastor Ellen warned us things can feel like they're at a standstill and then there'll be a sudden flurry of activity."

"We've sent three gifts since May," Paul wrote to Karl. "We're down to $11, so your donations are both welcome and timely." Karl was so good at encouraging others that Paul wondered what heartening information he could send in return for Karl to share with the Americans. In the absence of hard news, he decided on a story:

At the end of August, I heard half a dozen interns assessing their three months at the BC location of a Christian environmental organization, A Rocha, with centres in fifteen or twenty countries. An English woman, perhaps age thirty, explained that she had previously worked for five years in London with an international development organization. Having travelled a little for her work, she showed a photo of herself in West Africa and then one in the interior of Brazil.

When she reached a photo of Syrian tents in the Bekaa Valley in Lebanon (inland from our family, but Lebanon is a small country), she lost her composure and teared up. After struggling in silence for an uncomfortable period, she simply moved on to her next slide. She continued with her presentation for a couple of minutes and then interrupted it to say hesitantly, "I'm sorry I wasn't able to talk about the Syrian refugees. It's the one place I've visited where I just couldn't see any hope."

Sometimes it seems to me that our refugee sponsorship is a ridiculously small effort compared to all the needs in the world. It couldn't proceed at a more glacial pace. But then I remember what a beacon of hope we are providing for five very real people. A Rocha's philosophy, much like that of the early church, is local, small scale, relational, and long term. This strikes me as a pretty good anthem for our sponsorship.

As for the smoke we sent your way, it can't have been any thicker than what I encountered a couple of summers ago when driving across Idaho from Glacier Park in Montana to Pullman, Washington.

Yoga

A few people slipped through the double doors immediately after the session ended, but close to a dozen were still in various stages of rolling up mats or pumping mint tea from a stainless steel carafe. This was the second class in All Saints' six-week experiment with offering Saturday morning yoga, one that had been advertised on its outdoor sign so that neighbours would know they were welcome to attend.

"Isn't yoga sort of weird for a church to be offering?" some in the congregation had asked. "Either you're promoting Indian spirituality or you're doing an entirely physical version of yoga that's essentially a fitness class."

"Well, I think Christians should consider supporting any world view that promotes gratitude and non-harming," came one response. "But as I understand it, the class is mainly about physical health: about flexibility and gentle strengthening. The Hebrews in the Old Testament had a better grasp of the mind–body connection than the early church did, because of the influence of cerebral Greek philosophy in New Testament times. Even if all we end up providing is an exercise class with friends, it might help get us out of our heads and away from our fixation with ideas. The church needs a more robust appreciation of what it means to be physical beings created from dust."

"I'm not so sure about that, but I'll think about it. Maybe there's something to what you're saying."

The original intent had actually been to foster quite a different type of change in the congregation. It was part of a denominational initiative to reorient congregations away from doing good things *for* people and towards doing good things *with* people. "For generations, we've acted as if the church has all the answers and knows best, sharing its light with less fortunate mortals who walk in darkness. Sometimes we do have answers, good answers, but often we don't. Sometimes we even know deep down that we don't, but won't admit it. A bit more humility and openness might serve us well. Maybe we should focus more on being learners than teachers, walking the path alongside others and not always trying to lead them."

The question in Pastor Ellen's mind was whether the Syrian refugee sponsorship would develop a *with* character or whether it would be do-gooders acting *for* people in need. The yoga class was intended as an exercise in simply being *with* people from outside the congregation in more than a superficial way, an exercise in doing so while operating unabashedly under the auspices of the church.

Half a dozen All Saints members already attended yoga classes elsewhere, at least on occasion. The growing number of yoga studios in the community and classes in city recreation centres attested to a desire for healthier, less stressed living. Here, perhaps, was an activity where people of faith, agnostics, and atheists might find common ground. There was only one way to find out, and hence a low-stakes experiment was now underway.

Judi was one of the newcomers to yoga. She caught Penny's eye. "That was so different from what I expected," she said. "I liked it a lot, even though I couldn't begin to do the forward folds with my legs anywhere near straight. I'm glad the instructor said that whatever range of motion is available to us will be sufficient to benefit from a posture."

"Yes, she's good," Penny said. "This is one of those occasions when it's worth it to pay for a professional."

Paul tipped his rolled mat on end and placed it on the carpet, leaning it against the side of a birch bookshelf. "Stay!" he commanded as it threatened to slump. When it finally flopped over, he marched away in disgust towards Judi and Shayla.

"Hey, Paul," Shayla said and then turned to Judi. "I think our refugee group needs to get together again."

"Why?" Paul asked. "Nothing's happening."

"Not here, no. But Lebanon's a different story."

"How so?"

"I'm often in touch with Leandra," Shayla began. "There'll be a few weeks with nothing, and then lots of texting. I don't know how much help she's getting with the translation, but I figure anything that's happening will help them get more comfortable in dealing with an English society."

Judi and Paul nodded. This was familiar territory.

Shayla continued. "I'm learning that Lebanon is now trying to push Syrians back into their own country. I can't say that I blame it, but it's hard to go back to a land of civil war. It's even harder for persecuted Christians to return when the dominant Muslim groups on both sides of the conflict are rather less than sympathetic to their plight."

"So should we try contacting our MP again to see if we can get the processing of their refugee application a more urgent priority?" Judi asked.

"Wouldn't hurt," Shayla said. "But I don't know if any threat to their health or safety is high enough for the fast track. We can only try.

"On top of all this, Leandra says her little job has disappeared. It was only casual work, but it was work. A Lebanese displaced her, and the dad can't work. And for some reason—perhaps pressure from Lebanon—the UN is no longer providing $150 per month. So now they're totally dependent on us and their relatives for income."

"What were you starting to tell me last week about schooling?" Paul asked. "It sounded like more bad news on top of what you've just told us."

Shayla sighed as she recollected the overseas situation. Another couple from the yoga class had drifted over to listen. "The kids go to some sort of a school that the UN runs. They attend for a while in the late afternoon and then seem to return in the evening. Apparently it's not very good quality. Hardly a surprise and perhaps education isn't the biggest problem. Rather, Leandra has some concern that it's not teaching good morality."

"I've been wondering what that might mean," Paul said. "If it's associated with the UN, I wouldn't have thought sectarian propaganda would be much of a danger."

"I don't know, either," a grey-haired bystander said. "I've only been on the periphery of this refugee thing, but if I were the mother of a young daughter—"

"A pretty young daughter," Shayla said. "A crazy pretty daughter."

"If I were the mother of a pretty young daughter in a place where money is exceedingly scarce and in a setting that attracts predators and traffickers at the best of times, I know what I'd be worried about. In fact, I'd be really scared."

"Retreating to their attic isn't a realistic alternative. Besides, they're already heartily sick of it."

"This is starting to take on overtones of hiding Jews during the Second World War. I know the facts are entirely different, but the emotional climate seems closer than I care to think about. I'd like this to be a good news story, of us holding our little candle of hope and everything eventually coming to a happy ending in Canada."

"That's not always the way it works. In fact, it hardly ever works out nicely. We might just manage to make things a bit less awful."

"I know, I know. That's why I so desperately wish it were otherwise."

The discussion concluded with some vague intentions to step up the fundraising. Claire, the yoga instructor, had packed her blankets and other props into a wheeled suitcase and was making her way to the door. Judi stepped forward to hold it open for her, and the rest of the group followed.

"See you next week."

Three days later, Shayla received a note from the MP's constituency assistant. The assistant said there had been no changes to report since her last enquiry of Immigration, Refugees and Citizenship Canada—but not to be alarmed because sometimes data entry gets backlogged and then all the changes are logged into the database at the same time. She noted that medical examination results were on file and would remain valid for all family members until March 2018. The disappointing news was that the standard processing time was now approximately sixteen months for Lebanon, not the twelve months (from December 2016) that the All Saints welcoming team had understood. It could be another half a year before the family arrived in Canada, and there was little anyone could do in the meantime but wait.

Movement

The first sentence in Shayla's email ended with three exclamation marks. The good news was that a Canadian immigration official had phoned Yamo to say that the family's next interview would be on October 31. Things were still progressing, albeit at a snail's pace to anyone unfamiliar with the refugee process. When Shayla contacted Leandra on WhatsApp the day after the interview, the news was even better: all the hurdles had been cleared. Leandra reported that she and Yamo had signed papers about paying their "wages" to Canada ("I believe she meant paying for their airline tickets," Shayla explained) and had been congratulated by the officials. The Mousas were told they would leave in just a few more weeks.

The emails began flying almost immediately to set up a meeting of the welcoming team. Pastor Ellen had been the first to respond, calling the news exciting and reminding the group that, based on All Saints' previous experience with Iraqi refugees, things could come together very quickly. "I don't need to remind you how difficult it is to find housing. You may need to explore areas a bit further away to find accommodation."

Mount Olivet was not far behind in responding to Shayla, with Karl reaching out to Benediction church to restart the financial preparations. He told Benediction's staff person, Gayle, that he thought it was time to trigger Benediction's $5,000 donation. "The cost of housing in the Vancouver area is shocking, so this entire amount may be needed to cover the first month's rent, security deposit, and basic furnishings." He ended by saying this was such an exciting time to welcome new brothers and sisters into our midst. "What a blessed Christmas season we'll all enjoy."

Despite the anxiety that the family might arrive in just two or three weeks' time, most of the All Saints welcoming team couldn't assemble on the day Shayla had proposed. Eventually a date was found and the mechanics of transferring funds from Benediction became the focus of attention.

The first question was who in Canada should receive the funds. The consensus was that the money should go directly to All Saints, rather than CLWR, so that the welcoming team could easily access start-up money before the family arrived. Regarding the means of moving money, Vicki said, "I'm sure there's a slick way of transferring money electronically, but with the border, I'm reminded of the saying that while it may be human to err, to really mess things up requires a computer." She suggested a low-tech money order, payable to All Saints, be sent by registered mail.

The partners in Seattle received only a fraction of the email flurry, but it didn't take them long to perceive that the emotional climate in Vancouver was heating up far too rapidly. Karl sent an empathetic message. "I understand the semi-panic. Please let us know what the Seattle folks can do to lessen your load. If there is a moving/painting/etc. party, we can likely provide some helping hands and warm hearts."

Rather than calling it a day and heading home after her late afternoon meeting, Pastor Ellen slipped back into her office to reflect on all that had happened in the past seventy-two hours. She worried how quickly anxiety had escalated and how easily she had been drawn into it. Although tired, she knew she wouldn't rest properly until she sent a more measured and reassuring message to the welcoming team.

She started by recounting a conversation she'd had the day before with a church member who worked with teen mothers. "Sandra is continually looking for housing for the mothers and has ideas about who may help us. She has offered to do a little sleuthing for us, beginning with realtors she knows." She suggested CLWR be contacted to ensure the Seattle money had been converted into Canadian funds so that it could begin to be disbursed immediately after the Mousas arrived. "Peace and blessings," she closed, "in the midst of this excitement and terror."

Ellen relaxed into her swivel chair. She surmised that the Alcoholics Anonymous meeting had begun because the shuffling in the distance had silenced. She leaned forward to peer out of her office door, across the rotunda. Through the sliver of an interior window in the sanctuary, all was dark and still. No message light blinked on her desk telephone. Her day had ended well.

Nesting Instinct

Despite all the past discussions, a sense of inadequacy and insufficient preparation haunted those who would be the most involved with the arrangements. Some handled their anxiety by plunging into action even before the welcoming team could convene to strategize next steps. This resulted in several days of hard work, rather than smart work.

Accommodation was clearly the most urgent need. Previous talk had clarified location and several other criteria, but no rental budget had been finalized. Nevertheless, a flurry of house hunting began. Penny kicked off the conversation. "When I first moved here from Edmonton, I house-sat a couple of large houses for three months. That was in the olden days, before people really used the internet, so I put an ad in the local papers. Maybe we could find somebody who's going south for a few months this winter."

Two days later, Shayla announced at the Sunday service, "We need you to spread through all your networks that we're looking for housing. Temporary housing might have to suffice. However, we want to get the three children into school as quickly as possible. So that the kids' lives don't get even more disrupted, we'd prefer to find permanent housing right from the start.

"The furniture and furnishings—toaster ovens and butcher block for knives—all that can wait. We need housing first. As for furnishings, we're simply compiling a list of things that people have offered to donate."

Shayla leaned into the black gooseneck microphone. "If you have a hard time selling the idea of refugees coming to live in people's homes, remember that they are some of the best-checked and best-referenced people in the world. They have passed terrorist, criminality, and medical screening. They're also funded for the first year. And there are churches behind them with people to help."

"I can't emphasize this strongly enough," Ellen reiterated as Shayla stepped aside. "Get the word out to everyone. You can just say, 'Hey, we've got a family coming. We don't know if they're going to be here in maybe two weeks. Do you know of any place for them to stay?' You never know how that request will spread. It's often through the web of connections that things are found.

"Well, that's that," Ellen concluded. "Receive now God's good word, O Saints of God. Please stand if you are able and receive a blessing." She waited while the congregation rose from their seats. She stretched her arms up at a forty-five degree angle, palms facing out. "Almighty God—Father, Son, and Holy Spirit—bless you now and forever. Amen."

During coffee after the service, Joanna caught Paul's eye and edged her way towards him. "Would you be a reference on my passport application?"

"I don't have a professional job title anymore. Do they still require somebody like a teacher or a dentist who would fear losing their licence if they lie about who you are?"

"No, you just have to guarantee that I've lived here for as long as I claim."

"Sure, let me know when you want me to sign. And since we're talking, and you now owe me, let me ask you about co-ops and refugees."

Joanna worked for a company that provided management services to non-profit, co-operative housing societies. Paul wanted to know if purchasing a share in a co-op might be a feasible housing strategy, especially since shareholders wouldn't have to fear evictions, rent hikes, or exploitation by landlords.

Joanna wrinkled her brow. "Maybe. There are a few suites that might be in their price range. They'd have to purchase a share at the beginning that would be refundable when they leave. Perhaps $2,000. Would they have that kind of money upfront?

"We could use some of the donation from Benediction in Seattle for that."

"That clears one hurdle. The big problem is availability. The waitlists can be huge, but I'll ask around. The process is to make an application once the family arrives and then they have to get approved by the co-op board. The national guideline is that school age kids of different sexes can't share a bedroom, so we'd be looking for a three-bedroom unit. The girls can share."

The emails flew over the next forty-eight hours as people reported apartment listings they'd found on numerous websites. They were looking at bargain accommodation, but nothing suitable seemed available for less than $1,500 a month, perhaps more than the family could afford.

The following excerpts are typical of the emails:

– Lesley (realtor) warned of scams on Craigslist and to be extremely cautious. Also, I've heard rumours that potential renters are providing landlords with a year's worth of rent in order to secure a place. I'm not saying this to scare anyone but to let people know that this is the situation.

– Even though our budget isn't limitless, and they've been living in horrible conditions, I really don't want to see our family live in something that can't be nice, even if we have to do a thorough clean up and paint. The neighbourhood has to be really safe too. There are certainly some sketchy areas where I wouldn't want to live and I think personal safety is extremely important!

– What areas? I like some neighbourhoods more than others, but there's nowhere around here where I feel unsafe. But then, I'm a guy.

– Maybe we should look at an Airbnb option for the short-term since we really don't know a timeline.

– A bonus of a rental complex is that there is a ready-made community with similar families. If we find a basement suite, it might be isolating.

Paul cringed, fearing that people were starting to run off madly in all directions. He tried to refocus their efforts towards what he and a couple of likeminded people were thinking: a sympathetic landlord or non-market housing in the range of $1,200 to $1,500 per month, preferably three bedrooms, good public transit, and close to shopping and schools. Everyone agreed they preferred a local location and the ability to stay long term.

Shayla took a different approach in her attempt to better ground some well-intentioned helpers. "If you saw the apartment building the Badawis live in, you would probably turn right around. People are extremely poor. The building is badly looked after, and drafty and cold in the winter." *Actually, a lot of new immigrants and refugees live like that*, she thought but didn't mention. "However, the kids made friends and connected with people they trust and do not feel 'poorer than.' The Badawis discussed moving to something nicer, but the kids refused to leave. Zrebar said fit and stable were more important than nice."

Paul contacted Canadian Lutheran World Relief to see if they could verify that the Mousas would be travelling to Canada within the next couple of weeks. They couldn't. The staff explained they were supposed to receive notice of the visa approval, and then the International Organization for Migration would make resettlement arrangements. The Canadian Immigration department was supposed to give about ten days' notice of when the refugees would arrive in Vancouver. Paul sent a note to the welcoming team. "So...it could be two weeks, but it could also be two months or more."

A breakthrough came on November 6 when Pastor Ellen received an email offering temporary housing for the family should nothing else be available. Because the couple making the offer would be sharing their house with the Mousas and not putting them in a separate suite, this was very much a fall-back position. They wanted this temporary safety net to last for no more than a month or two. For fear that their offer might lead to reduced house hunting efforts, they asked to remain anonymous for the time being and the offer not be publicized.

"This certainly is a relief," Ellen wrote. Now that the immediate pressure had lessened, Ellen wanted to help the congregation better consider newcomers' perspectives, rather than viewing needs through a North American lens. After pondering the topic for a few minutes, she decided that first tugging at the heartstrings might be effective.

"Let's ensure that people from Seattle get to the airport to welcome the family when they arrive. It will have to be low key because the family will be exhausted and overwhelmed, but I can say that it will be a profoundly moving experience for everyone." She described how a few weeks earlier, when the Badawi family became Canadians citizens, they all vividly recalled their arrival. "Zrebar still weeps when she talks about walking through the door. We brought them 'Canada' mittens that remain precious mementos of their arrival."

She continued, saying that often the first response of North Americans looking to support refugees concerns material things: furnishings to be donated or places for newcomers to live. Upon a moment's reflection, the focus frequently switches to job possibilities and schooling. The assumption—a weak one—is that the newcomers will be entirely happy to have arrived in Canada and eager to learn Canadian ways. "In reality, the emotional and psychological complexities are more difficult to anticipate than physical considerations and even harder to address."

The partners in Seattle were more than willing to help with the full range of needs, but they recognized the limitations of distance. At this particular moment, their help might have to be restricted to shopping and physical items. Karl summarized the current conundrum in Seattle. In addition to the online spreadsheet the Canadians had posted about donations and needed furniture, did it make sense for the Americans to do some shopping at an international retailer such as IKEA or use an Amazon gift registry? A conference telephone call seemed the most effective way to sort out the specifics about shopping.

When the call occurred, Shayla reiterated her concern about sustainability. "We don't want to set them up for feelings of failure and disruption after the first year when the sponsorship ends. They don't need fancy. Also, Paul, do you remember when we set up the Badawis' pantry?"

Paul thought for a moment. "Uh, no, not really."

"We had a food drive at the church when they first arrived," Shayla said. "We brought the Badawis to the church one weekday morning to meet a few of us and then loaded up a car with all the food we'd collected. We meant well, but it turned out that we totally humiliated them because they were visibly seen to be objects of charity. They come from a culture where honour is important, so we should have been discrete with our gifts. On top of that, we hadn't been sensitive to the dietary restrictions of their religion since we had never even heard of halal, nor had we researched their regional cuisine to find out what they might prefer to eat."

"I'm getting it," Gayle said. "We need energetic helpers, but ones who are sensitive and at least partially informed."

"Yes," Paul said. "Here's another potential complication. I don't know if it's likely, but it's at least a possibility. Suppose the Mousas arrive with survivor's guilt. Here they are in Canada. No matter how scary it might be, they have the possibility of a better life. In contrast, some of their friends and family are living in tents, perhaps being pushed out of Lebanon and back into the war zone in Syria. But the Mousas have arrived to a safe, warm, well-furnished place. Our good intentions could backfire if we just reinforce their guilt."

"Really?" Karl asked sceptically.

"I don't know," Paul replied. "I'm just saying we need to be thinking about these possibilities."

Paul tossed and turned in bed that evening, wondering if the Vancouver people had been sourpusses when they urged so much caution. He feared he had come across as ungrateful. Surely he and Shayla could have found something more constructive to say, something that would better enable Seattle to contribute actively to the preparations.

The next morning, he proposed searching for a used tablet or two while the support group figured out the family's skill and needs with respect to computers. "I'm thinking a tablet rather than a laptop because it's so easy to switch keyboards between Arabic and English. I'm thinking Apple—am I allowed to mention that company to people who live so close to Microsoft in Redmond?— because we have an Apple store near our church and their service desk will often do basic troubleshooting for free."

When the welcoming team finally convened later in the week, the tone was relaxed because of the anonymous offer of a temporary place for the Mousas to stay. Amelia Hilborn, who had been part of the All Saints contingent that visited Mount Olivet almost a year ago, had accepted the invitation to attend this meeting—an invitation that was extended without knowing she had offered the temporary accommodation. Because the first issue they wanted to resolve was the maximum rent they could afford, the group decided to set a preliminary budget.

"The child tax benefit might take up to six months to come through," Amelia clarified, "but it's retroactive, I think it's safe to budget $4,200 a month, rather than $2,900 without the grants."

Hearts sank when the public transit website showed the cost of a monthly pass was $93 to $172 for an adult, depending on the number of zones. While children could get unlimited travel for $53 per month, transportation for the family was likely going to cost between $350 and $500 per month.

Could a family of five buy sufficient groceries on $200 a week and eat only home-cooked food prepared from scratch for every single meal each month? No, the allowance would have to be higher. Okay, would $300 a week be sufficient, assuming purchases of expensive items like meat and dairy were minimized? The uncertainty about the cost of food brought home the reality of living in poverty and the freedom from worry of everyday life in the middle class life.

As the group considered what were necessities, the conversation drifted towards the ways in which foreigners do not always perceive or value things the way Canadians do. "Let's face it," Judi said, "squat toilets are apparently common in the Middle East. If that's what our family is accustomed to, then no matter how nice the bedspreads and lamps, they may find their housing somewhat disgusting because they have to wipe their bottoms with little pieces of dry paper. Why, they may think, doesn't their new host country follow the more hygienic technique of using water?"

"Even arriving at the Vancouver airport might not be the happy occasion we envision," Vicki said.

"No," Amelia said. "When the Badawis arrived five years ago, the kids were exhausted and crying. The airport in Damascus was being bombed when they began their long flights to Canada. Then in Vancouver, immigration officials had to process them before an officer escorted them out the international arrivals gate. We even had to sign for them."

"Then, I suppose, it took some organizing to bring them home?" Paul asked.

"Yes," Amelia replied. "We loaded them in separate vehicles, one for males and the other for females, so that we weren't mixing the sexes. This probably won't be a religious requirement for our new family, but perhaps it will be a cultural expectation."

"Oh, my brain is starting to hurt." Judi raised her hands to her head, wincing and grinning slightly. "I've reached my evening's threshold for thinking. Maybe it's time to schedule another meeting."

Furnishings and Snail Mail Money

The high-priority message from Shayla said that a colleague's church in a nearby town, after outfitting their Syrian family with an entire household, was offering an "almost new" double bed and matching dresser to All Saints. "The catch is that the donor can't hold on to the furniture. She needs to know ASAP if we want it and can pick it up." The issue, in Shayla's view, was not whether the welcoming team wanted the furniture but whether anyone had space to store it.

Amelia replied quickly that she could store it. A second offer came from a young woman who suggested pressuring her parents. "They have a large basement and they also could store some of it under their covered deck—though not the mattress or any of the soft items, of course."

"Thank you, Amelia," Shayla wrote. "Now we just need a few dry hours and a pick-up truck. Who has connections?"

A scant forty-eight hours later, another offer of furniture arrived, this time from Benediction church in Seattle. It came embedded in a message from Gayle, the church staff person, saying she was about to send $5,100 US to All Saints by registered mail.

Paul expressed his thanks, mentioning that, having heard nothing more from Lebanon, he expected the funds would arrive well ahead of the family. He signalled that he really didn't expect the family anytime soon and was cautious about accepting big furniture that might have to be stored for weeks or months. "So we're back in lurch-forward-then-wait mode. The strange resignation of the Lebanese prime minister adds one more uncertainty, given the volatility of Lebanon at the best of times." Others at All Saints were less reticent than Paul.

While the furniture—or at least the offers—were streaming in, the mail from Seattle was decidedly sluggish. The Canadians fussed that neither the American nor Canadian post office tracking websites disclosed what had happened after the envelope reached the Canadian customs agency. After almost three weeks, Shayla felt she had to let Gayle know the money still hadn't arrived, hastening to reassure her, "I think things are probably on track but going terribly slowly, consistent with everything else having to do with the sponsorship."

"Borders are so annoying," Karl wrote from Seattle. He evidently was not concerned. "Back in October when we thought it was 'any day now,' a bunch of people donated spontaneously. I've mailed a check for $750 US to be used as needed—for continuing support in Lebanon, travel costs, or resettlement expenses." He did, however, ask to be informed of any delay in receiving his letter. The letter arrived at the church office just a couple of days later.

After checking the tracking websites daily about Benediction's mail, Paul eventually saw that customs officials had finally released the envelope to Canada Post. He told Gayle that her post had reached Canada, after first travelling the opposite direction to San Francisco, within four days. Then the Canada Border Services Agency held and opened the envelope for two weeks. After two unsuccessful delivery attempts at the church when no staff were present to sign for the registered letter, Paul finally picked it up on December 9 at the neighbourhood postal outlet. "This has been an eye opener for me, helping me better appreciate how cumbersome overseas refugee processing must be. I'm glad we're not doing anything unusual or complicated."

Penny happened to see Paul after service the following Sunday. "So the border people held on to the envelope for over two weeks. Was this just Christmas backlog or did they inspect it?"

"They opened both the priority post package and the envelope inside it with the cheques and letter."

"Given the way security people share intelligence, I guess that means, if we weren't already on the radar of Homeland Security in the United States, we probably are now. What a sad situation that ordinary people who are trying to do some good may now start to worry whether they'll be watched or questioned when they cross the border."

Bring on the Bishops

With the kids finally in bed, Shayla cleared her throat and glared at her husband. "Do not. Under any circumstances. Interrupt me. For the next hour." She stuck out her tongue. "Maybe for the entire week."

"Love you, too," he murmured as he placed the kettle on its base and reached for a handcrafted mug.

"Thanks, sweetie. I'm days behind on my email and simply need a block of time to get caught up."

"Quit dawdling, then, and get to work. I'm giving you exactly sixty minutes before becoming unmercifully needy." He broke eye contact and studiously opened a package of chamomile tea, ignoring her as she made her way to the computer desk.

One of her incoming emails was a word of encouragement from Lori-Ann. Shayla dithered whether to invite her family to read the section where Lori-Ann said she was impressed by All Saints' organizing, but decided against it—she knew she'd be ribbed endlessly every time something went wrong. *As it all too frequently does*, she thought.

On the other side of town, Paul dithered whether to tell SRAG about a potential development in early January because it was so tentative. He would have preferred more solid information, but with the disruption of the upcoming Christmas holidays, he decided that early notice would be advisable. "Bishops from our respective denominations, the Evangelical Lutheran Church in America and the Evangelical Lutheran Church in Canada, are coming to Vancouver at the beginning of January for some sort of gathering. Rumour has it that a contingent of said clerics—Canada has only half a dozen bishops, while the US has over sixty—is likely to come to All Saints on January 7 for Sunday morning worship. This would be a wonderful opportunity for us to tell our story of our cross-border partnership."

Paul saved the message in his draft folder and flopped on a couch to consider whether to also share the news about Pastor Ellen. He flipped through a coffee table book, hoping his subconscious mind would process his dilemma. It didn't. He returned to his Mac computer and resumed his email. "Pastor Ellen Thompson has just accepted a call from the BC Synod to shift from half time to full time as assistant to the bishop for missional renewal and congregational care." He suggested that with her impending departure, she would all the more cherish any who came to the service with the bishops.

I guess it's fair to try and guilt them into coming, Paul thought, *since the January weather can be frightful for travelling. I'm just evening the odds of a decent attendance.* He ended with an accounting of all the small donations, totalling $2,000, for overseas support of the Mousas that had arrived in the past twelve months.

Amy Cassidy was the first from Seattle to accept the invitation. "Please count me in! I so enjoyed our visit last time: the fellowship of the 'big family' style evening supper, the game with the children, and the worship together and lunch on Sunday."

Lori-Ann had rather a different, although positive, response. "Also, an odd question: Is there a WiFi connection at the church or somewhere nearby? My son and I are scheduled to lead a meeting with youth in Seattle. I'm wondering if we might do it by Skype from Canada?"

Paul replied that he thought the church had WiFi but wasn't sure how trustworthy it was. "However, I live only a mile away. I'd suggest trying to connect from both locations on Saturday night to ensure you have a backup option, and then decide on Sunday which location you want to use."

Within a week, All Saints received confirmation that two or three carloads of guests from the Bishop's Academy, a five-day educational and consultative event, would be attending worship on January 7. The entourage, as Vicki described it, would consist of a random mixture of bishops, some spouses, and perhaps a staff person or two. Best of all, not only would a description of the refugee project be welcome, the entire sermon could be devoted to it.

"Let's start with telling them how the sponsorship came about in the first place," Judi suggested. "It's a fascinating story, and I don't think even most people at All Saints know it. Then a couple of other people could speak about other things."

"Like what?" Pastor Ellen asked. She enthusiastically supported lay people telling their stories but wanted to ensure there would be no gaffs with so many dignitaries present.

Judi proposed the theme could be that God was already using a family of five Syrians to touch the lives of over fifty North Americans. "They're changing the ways we view the world, reducing the isolation created by a border along the 49th parallel, and helping us pay more attention locally to how we welcome and include newcomers."

"Sounds good to me," agreed Ellen. "The Scripture readings are about the Spirit of God hovering over the formless void in the creation story in Genesis, followed by the New Testament reading about the Spirit descending on Jesus when he was baptized by John the Baptist. It shouldn't be hard to make the connection about the Spirit at work in this refugee sponsorship."

As attention shifted to the logistics of the weekend, an unexpected offer energized the group: a husband and wife from All Saints volunteered to cook a Sunday morning breakfast at the church for the Seattle visitors, the welcoming team and any choir members who were coming early to rehearse for the service. "We've prepared lots of breakfasts for big groups over the years," they said. "It's our specialty. We won't need any help."

The potluck lunch for the entire congregation and the bishops would entail more work, but the casualness planned for the previous evening's gathering with the Seattle guests would balance this effort. The idea for Saturday night was simply to gather for conversation and a few light nibbles. It might not even be a late evening because it looked like at least one Seattle visitor was going to accept the offer from an All Saints family to ski with them on Mount Seymour for a few hours—hard daytime skiing might mean an early bedtime. Now that friendships had been established, organizing homestays for the anticipated half dozen Americans was no effort at all.

Saturday Evening Conversation

The tables in All Saints' foyer varied in length. They had been pushed together to form a slightly irregular square. Only a few red tablecloths could be located in the kitchen cupboards resulting in the centre table sporting a light green and white plaid instead. None of these irregularities mattered because the appetizers and desserts arriving with the five visitors from Seattle and the dozen locals were equally haphazard.

Hugs were exchanged as familiar faces drifted into the room, while handshakes remained the norm for introductions. Eventually the conversation clusters made their way to the tables, seating themselves on the perimeter as platters of food circulated, some passed to the left, some to the right, and some stalled.

"We don't have an agenda," Judi explained to the group. "Nor do we have any topics that we have to cover this evening. A lot of time has passed since our two churches got together, so this is an opportunity to exchange news and ask questions. It's all wide open. What's on your mind?"

Ninety minutes of relaxed conversation ensued. Side conversations periodically developed but they were discreet and brief, and the group essentially ran itself. Here is a sampling of the evening's conversations:

Challenges Facing Newcomers
– Did the family that All Saints sponsored five years ago ever say what was the most difficult thing in adapting to Canada? Was it language?

– It's the mother, Zrebar, who I know best. She never complained, although I know she had some difficulty adjusting to the Canadian economic and social services systems. In Iraq, when Saddam Hussein was in power, it was a top-down society. She was part of the privileged minority. They got free schooling and free health care, gas was cheap, and life was good. So moving from a country that meets your needs, albeit a totalitarian country, to a country where good things also happen, but where the less privileged have to scrape for so much, was a hard adjustment. It's not that they weren't willing to work hard, it's just that some groups in Canadian society seem to encounter more roadblocks than others. In Canada, her family was one of the groups facing barriers.

She never really said that, though, or said anything bad. That was my interpretation. She just said, "We're so glad we're safe. We would have slept on a concrete floor, knowing there's no bombs and we're not going to get abducted. Nobody's going to get killed and nobody's going to get tortured. What more can I ask for? My kids are safe and God will help us."

– The reality is that it can get even harder later for refugees. Refugee families could have even more difficult years ahead of them. Sometimes we just have to say to parents, "You've done this for your children. Canada can't offer you a good life. The sad reality is that you'll probably always have subsistence living."

– Plus, what they've been through has probably scarred them badly. There are daily disappointments and each day gets a little harder when you don't have all that you need or want for your family. It takes a long time to plough through all those bad, bad feelings. Kids catch up, though.

Role of Children
– I've belonged to two churches in Seattle. The two have sponsored a combined total of at least seven families, mostly Asian. In the long run, we found one of the really hard things was that the children become more adept than the parents.

It switched the power dynamic in the family. It was the children who had to help make decisions; they were the ones who helped interpret papers because they learned English faster than their parents did. The kids ended up being the power brokers in the family, and the parents fell behind. It cost the parents a lot to lose their position in the family.

Then the children became so Americanized. There was dating and so on, and the parents lost control of the children's social lives. It was hard for the parents as the children adjusted to their new world.
– Yes, I've seen this personally because I have a son who I adopted as a seventeen year old. He came alone from Cambodia and ended up living with us. When he eventually married and had children, it was his children who were the more competent ones in the family. My son is fifty-four years old now. He's not in good health, and he doesn't handle life very well. His son still sometimes has to read for him, explaining complex documents. Very hard for the parents.

Relationships with Others
– There are so many opportunities for relationships. They're going to need dinner invitations and shopping trips. This kind of a

Saturday night informal get together, perhaps with some games—though maybe not *Trivial Pursuit*. There's no limit to how close our relationships could be and how many people they can connect with.

– But there will be one relationship that can't be replicated and that's with whoever first meets them, the first responders. That place of trust is priceless. Most of us are not going to know every personal detail about the family, nor should we expect to know. They'll probably bond with one or two people, and it's only those people who will be privy to the intimate details of the family's lives. The rest of us will be in layers and ripple out.

– One immigrant family told me that, in their language, they have no word for friend. They don't need friends because the extended family is everything, their tribe. Jumping across the ocean, they lost their connections, so we became their family. Family forgives each other. Family stays connected. We're in it for these people for much longer than one year.

Safe Spaces

– I remember a Saturday night gathering with our first refugee family. There at the table were two families, one from Iran and one from Iraq. That would never have happened back in their part of the Middle East. Back home, the hatred was expected. Here, we were able to provide a safe space for them to explore something different.

– Some of you have heard this story before, but I find it so powerful. It's also something that happened in this building. An American, an Iraqi, and a Canadian woman were sitting together in a small cluster at the back of the room. The Iraqi woman spoke of the terror she felt as the American soldiers came around the corner in her village. The American woman was shocked, having only ever perceived her troops as heroes, the good guys, never imagining that people, ordinary people, would be frightened by their presence. And the Canadian woman was holding space, creating a safe place where a conversation like this could take place.

The kicker for me is that, all the while, the pre-teen Iraqi and American boys and girls were romping around playing tag and hide-and-go-seek. They weren't part of that awful history. That's how enlightened immigration policy can help change the world.
– On a more mundane level, we can encourage their learning of English with our relationships because the safer they feel, the more likely they'll risk making the mistakes that are inevitable in learning any language.

Role of Sponsors
– In this sponsorship, everything we do is with the family, not for them. That means we're respecting their integrity and adulthood, not treating them as children. We want to give them as many ways to be making their own decisions as we can.
The flip side of this is that it's important to be brutally honest. It's not helpful to hold off telling them about the reality of something. We need to be able to say, "It's your decision, but be aware that if you do X, here's the potential effect on Y." In the end, it has to be their choice, but it's our responsibility as sponsors to give them reliable information about how our society works.
– We want them to outfit their home with things they know they really will use. I've worked in kitchens where there were things I never used. It could be that they'll never use a toaster. They're not going to need a complete set of silverware. But a pile of spoons and a pile of soup bowls from Value Village might be a perfect start for the way they cook. We'll need to let them choose the things they want to live with.
– It's not helpful to start them off with a middle-class lifestyle they won't be able to keep up in the long run. We can all remember sleeping on a foamy, and then the pride of being able to move up to a futon. As your means improve, the stuff comes along.
The stuff is not what's going to make a huge difference to a successful integration into Canadian society. At this point, it's now

better to have money so they can pay bus fares and so on. And they need relationships, ones that support and enable new Canadians to find their way.

Practical Matters

- I love the phrase used with our previous refugee sponsorship: messy but beautiful. This family isn't going to be perfect, any more than ours are. We may think we're prepared, but no...oops. They'll come with a whole different set of issues.

- The dentist I go to, he goes back to Iraq regularly and provides free care. We can start asking around for dentists who do pro bono work. The interesting thing, though, is that all the dentists are doing it already.

- Muslims, as part of their faith, are not allowed to charge interest. So that means they cannot take on a mortgage. That's why some foundations have been formed to gather money that can be loaned at zero percent interest to enable Muslims to purchase homes.

- I just pray that our messages to and from Lebanon are encrypted and private.

Getting It Wrong

- Do you remember when somebody told us that Middle Easterners use lots of thyme in their cooking? We thought we'd be helpful and rushed out to buy a bunch of ground thyme. When we presented it, they just looked bewildered. It turned it out that it's the fresh herb they use, not the jar of mystery powder. We were doing something that made us feel good but that didn't meet the actual need because we lacked information. We were doing things for people, rather than with them.

- Without regular payments to Lebanon, we're having to balance how to be helpful without being disruptive. We know the money is getting to the family okay, but we don't know if there's somebody standing at the door when they walk out of the Western Union office asking for their cut. Pastor has a story from her time in the Ukraine about a kid who didn't have any shoes. She bought him a pair of shoes. The next day he was barefoot again, but now he had a black eye.

– That reminds me of the time I lived in Africa. There was a man with some mental problems, perhaps in his twenties or thirties. He would often dance around our houses, close to the hospital and school where the Westerners lived. He frequently didn't have pants. He might have a shirt but not trousers. So somebody would fit him with some trousers. A few days later, he'd show up again and he'd still not be wearing pants. So somebody else would say, "We've got to get pants on this man."

We were outfitting his whole family. He'd get home and they'd take the pants away and send him our way again. It took a long time for us to realize we weren't helping him at all. His family, yes, and maybe that was a good thing—or maybe not. The point is we really weren't accomplishing what we thought we were.

Help from Seattle
– In terms of your help to us here in Vancouver, I still think the most powerful contribution you in Seattle have made is to energize us so we can do the hands-on things. We can get up and talk to others in our congregation, but it's like listening to your mother's instructions. When an outsider, however, makes a trip, crosses a border, stays overnight, and gives a lot of money to all this, it catches our attention and energizes the whole congregation.

Just knowing we have to send you messages and be accountable to you—oh, gee, we haven't done anything recently—prods us to get moving. Emotional support isn't the right word. It's your interest, the doing things together. You're both a safety net and an encouragement.

– We in Seattle get the same from you.

Preach It, Sister

Penny took her time at the lectern, surveying the assembly of worshippers before she started speaking. "The first verse in the Bible is famous. In the beginning, God created the heavens and the earth. The second verse is a touch harder to recall." She spoke more deliberately now. "The earth was a formless void and darkness"—she emphasized darkness before continuing—"covered the face of the deep, while a wind from God swept over the face of the waters."

She paused. "Darkness and water and chaos, and the hovering Spirit are central in today's sermon."

After an even longer pause, Penny resumed in a lighter tone. "I'm going to set the stage for the next speaker by giving you a slightly fictionalized account, with some names changed, of a true story. More precisely, I'll share the beginning of a long and ongoing story."

She gazed across the congregation, noticing two of the five bishops, men from Florida and British Columbia, seated near the back. "On September 3, 2015, the newspaper image of three-year-old Alan Kurdi's body, prostrate and partially submerged on a beach in Turkey, galvanized the world to the plight of Syrians." She happened to glance at the third row where the national American bishop, Sandra Andersen, sat with her husband. Sandra nodded her head slightly, as she recalled the photograph. Penny went on to recount the origins of the Syrian refugee sponsorship, a story which became the first chapter of this book.

"Well, the Canadians agreed to the proposed partnership. The Americans kept their promise. Eventually Canadian Lutheran World Relief told us we had been assigned a family of five. That family is still in exile in Lebanon. They've passed their health and security checks and could arrive any week now."

"Two years this has taken. Two years and they're still displaced in the Middle East.

"All we've accomplished in two years," Penny thundered, "is to send some piddling stipends to help with living expenses."

181

Disdain did not come naturally to Penny, but she felt she was not doing too badly. "When the family does arrive, they'll just be a drop in the refugee bucket. Maybe they'll flourish; maybe they won't. But bringing people to new countries and new cultures isn't a viable, large-scale remedy for the world's traumas, especially when we have so many unmet needs here at home."

She knew she had the full attention of the congregation because there wasn't a sound as she prepared for her final thrust. "So what's the point?"

She paused, looking around at the congregation.

"Is taking in a few refugees just tokenism to make some North Americans feel good while avoiding our responsibility to help keep other parts of the world healthy and safe?" She dropped her eyes and almost whispered, "It's not hard to see darkness on the face of the deep." Her shoulders slumped as she stepped aside to let Shayla come forward. The congregation remained very still.

Shayla began. "What can I text or email to a family who is cold, hungry, afraid, without jobs, and having to sponge off relatives? Living in one room, experiencing the tension that comes from overcrowding, poverty, and boredom. Waiting to be accepted into Canada so that their lives may continue without harassment, in peace, with a future for their children, with meaning?" She finally lifted her eyes from her notes.

"I want to say that things will be much better here, but I'm acutely aware of our housing crisis and the thousands of British Columbians without a dignified roof over their heads.

"I want to say their children will be safe, well cared for and free from persecution, but then I remember the attacks on the worshippers in the mosque in Quebec City last February, racist leaflets in Vancouver neighbourhoods, and a sense of complacency about sharing our wealth with those less fortunate.

"I want to say they will find work, yet I know how hard it can be for immigrants to write their résumés, be considered for an interview, acquire language, fend off depression.

"A few days ago, I asked our Syrian mom to describe how the children are doing, what they like, how their learning is going. This is her reply. 'I don't know what to say. In the past, I used to get my kids CDs of church liturgy, but now we are just counting down the days when we will finish with this toxic environment. The kids aren't going to school anymore.'

"I asked what had happened and apologized that we can't speed up the process for them. She said, 'Nothing happened, but my husband and I have no work and we can no longer pay the bus fare to school. We are fine and pray for you, and thank God for everything.'

"And yet, despite the struggles they will definitely face once they're here,"—Shayla drew back her shoulders—"I live in the hope that through the work of so many of us, which ultimately I cannot explain other than that this is God's work in action, we may come to help this family."

She smiled gently. "I have come to trust this process, partly because our Iraqi-Canadian friends have already contributed more to Canadian society through their volunteering than some who were born here many years earlier. Their giving back over the past five years helps to improve Canadian society and enables others to succeed.

"Whenever I get overwhelmed by the prospect of helping another family figure out their new life in a strange land, I am reminded that I am not alone." She searched the congregation until she found a few visitors from Seattle. "Others have walked this path before us and are willing to help. Our Seattle friends have helped me learn that a lack of expertise or confidence need not stop me from attempting to make life better for others."

Now Shayla was smiling broadly. "Whenever the figure of 62 million refugees worldwide threatens to turn me off the topic

BOB COWIN

altogether, I just send another text to Lebanon and ask how our sisters and brothers are doing—that is indeed what they call us.

"Whenever I have the feeling that in this rich world I am being handed the short stick and am entitled to more, I look at the children's latest photos from Lebanon. I make a few phone calls so we can pick up our fundraising efforts, our furniture collections, our sponsorship group meetings again to prepare for the day when we drive to the airport to welcome them with open arms."

She shrugged and shook her head ruefully. "This tiny drop in the refugee bucket has gotten under my skin. In a good way. Against all odds. And for the better."

Penny and Shayla slowly exchanged places.

"I told you a moment ago," Penny said, "that it isn't hard for me to see darkness and chaos. What I didn't tell you, but which I want to say now, is that I also sense the hovering Spirit telling me, 'Look, look again. Look at how this family of five Syrians, whom you have yet to meet, has already touched and changed dozens of North Americans.'

"This family already knows what it means to depend totally on God. Maybe the work of the Spirit in this refugee sponsorship is every bit as much about transforming the lives of the sponsors and, through them, nudging their communities deeper into the Kingdom of God."

She let her point sink in, namely that caring for refugees can lead privileged Westerners into a more fulfilled and authentic way of living. "Shayla's is just one of the stories of how the Spirit has been at work among us through this refugee sponsorship, a sponsorship that has yet to be birthed. Stories of how the brief life of one toddler in the Middle East is rippling out across the continents to not only touch people's lives but to actually change them. Stories of how God is at work to transform our lives, perhaps yours but certainly mine."

FINAL PREPARATIONS

Arriving Soon

Shayla eagerly spread the word that Canadian authorities had contacted the Mousa family in early January, asking first if they were in good health and then advising that they would be travelling soon. "Our thoughts and prayers may have achieved something," Shayla rejoiced. "It's as if our meeting sent shock waves around the world. This is the time to get ready. They may get the go-ahead any day now!" The next step would be for the authorities to provide visas and travel details.

A couple of days later, the office of the member of Parliament phoned Shayla to confirm that things were progressing well. In doing their regular twelve-week check-in with the immigration department in Ottawa, the office had learned that all the checks had been successfully completed. "Let's take the Mousas to meet the office assistant after they arrive here," Shayla suggested.

"And to the CLWR office," Judi added.

As the jubilation waned, the welcoming team turned its attention to the inevitable logistical concerns. "I just want to remind you," Amelia said, "that if the family arrives in the last half of January, my husband and I will be out of town. They're still welcome to stay in our house when they arrive even if we aren't there."

The team designated Paul to keep the key to Amelia's home for that two-week period. Not only did he live relatively close by, but his schedule was flexible. "I can even sleep there if needed, commuting between Amelia's place and mine," he offered.

Amelia and Paul arranged an evening for him to pick up the house key and receive an orientation—a rather important orientation because the interior had recently been renovated and was rather more high tech than Paul felt comfortable handling. "Just show me the simplest cold-water wash cycle," he pleaded, "and whether there's another garbage container we could use so that I don't have to figure out what to do when the battery-operated lid stops functioning."

"I guess you only want to learn how to connect to one of the four WiFi networks in the house?" Amelia asked. "Actually, I get confused, too. That's what happens when your son-in-law works for a telecommunications company."

"Oh, I wouldn't be surprised if the Mousas can figure out WiFi on their own. It's all these other gadgets and ultra-programmable thermostats that are likely to give us grief. I really hope they don't arrive until after you're back."

"Relax. I'll occasionally check my email while we're away. And they're survivors."

"That's fine for you to say. I'm dealing with so much information overload I can barely remember what bedroom you said you'd assigned to which family member."

"The only absolutely essential thing you have to remember to tell them is to keep the shower curtain inside the bathtub so we don't have a flood. They might come from one of those places with tiled bathrooms that have no separate shower stalls. You know, the ones with flex showerheads you hold in your hand and Westerners end up soaking the entire bathroom, including all the toilet paper."

Paul nodded ruefully. "Hmmm. I suppose I'll also need to find a way to tell them that, in Canada, once toilet paper has served its purpose, it's always flushed and doesn't ever go in the waste basket. Not all places do it the Western way."

"Unless it's wrapping a pad or dabbing cosmetics. Don't look so pained, Paul. You'll do fine."

January 24, 2018
Shayla to the welcoming team and SRAG:

> Leandra Mousa and family will be FLYING TO CANADA ON MARCH 6!

> ALL HANDS ON DECK FROM NOW ON! Please let us know how you can assist in your own small or larger way.

> Thanks be to God!

Equally excited, Penny's reply also shouted in uppercase letters. "I'M SITTING IN MY OFFICE AT WORK WITH TEARS STREAMING DOWN MY FACE."

After a few more hallelujahs, the Seattle folk started making plans. "Your American partners are on call," Karl wrote. "Once the All Saints core team gathers its wits, let's have a conference call to see how we can be most useful." Almost as an afterthought, he mentioned that he would like to come up. "But I will coordinate with the other Americans to make sure we don't overwhelm."

"Like to come? I think he's dying to come," Judi commented. "But that's typical of him and William—willing to stay in the background. We absolutely have to get them to the airport."

Paul forwarded all this correspondence to Amelia, the temporary innkeeper, because she had been overlooked in the distribution list. *Thank goodness,* he thought, *I'm off the hook to be the caretaker at her house.*

The next day, Shayla urged serious hunting for permanent housing to begin right away. "They'll have to give an address for several important documents, including school registration, during the first days of their arrival. It's such a hassle to change addresses, and perhaps schools, and it's more work for everybody." She was also eager that the children get registered in school in the few days before spring break. Another portion of her email reminded the team of all the things to be organized. "Shopping at Value Village," it began and ended with "invite the kids swimming, explain how the sewing machine works, play LEGO with Semir, teach busing, get a cell phone plan, buy gum boots, gather Syrian food staples or take them grocery shopping, walk the neighbourhood."

Despite not yet having an official notice of the arrival date, the group wanted to find permanent accommodation that would be available in March. The money from Benediction could be used to pay the first month's rent. It wasn't clear who would sign the tenancy and pay the deposit to hold a suite for the Mousas, but that could be sorted out later. They started yet another round of discussions about the rental budget, with little prospect of reaching consensus.

Home Sweet Home

Shayla wasted no time in scouring rental websites in the forlorn hope that, this time, she would find something both suitable and affordable. Several hours into her search, she leaned forward in her chair. A ground-level suite with three bedrooms not too far from where she lived looked promising. She phoned the landlord, a young woman who had recently acquired and renovated the house as an investment property. "The landlord didn't seem shocked about having refugees as tenants," she later said to Judi. "Rather, she seemed quite pleased that we would be doing something nice for others."

Shayla enquired about three other properties but didn't hear back. "I did learn that communities a further twenty or thirty minutes away from downtown aren't any cheaper."

Judi immediately looked up the address on Google Maps. "This is a great location. Very central for all the schools the kids need to attend, five- to twenty-minute walks. And they can go on foot to town for shopping and the recreation centre. The only thing I don't like is that there's only one bathroom. Otherwise perfect."

Vicki gave a tentative thumbs up. "It's a bit of a gamble in that we don't have an official arrival date—things can still unravel—but I think it's worth the risk."

The next day, four team members huddled after church to arrange to meet the landlord at the suite later in the afternoon. Arriving individually at the address over a ten-minute period, they found the neighbourhood to be ordinary, made up of modest, mainly vinyl-sided houses dating from the 1980s. The street was wide and quiet, making for easy parking.

"Hello, I'm Parvan," a slender woman with long, dark hair said, extending her hand.

"I'm Vicki. I'm sorry, I didn't quite catch your name. Barpin?"

"Parvan. Rhymes with car van."

"Oh, that helps," Judi said. "This is Shayla." Sweeping her arm a little to the left, she continued. "And Paul and Vicki. I'm Judi."

Parvan unlocked the double-wide front door, ushering the group onto the landing for the stairs to the top floor. "The upstairs tenants are a young family with two children." She reached for an interior door handle and led the group into the laundry room.

"Nice new machines," Judi whispered.

"This is a walkthrough laundry room that the two suites share," Parvan explained. "Each door has a different lock, so the tenants can't get into each other's place. We came in the door for the upstairs suite. I'll show you the side entrance for the ground suite in a moment."

One wall in the combined kitchen and living area was yet to be painted. A thin film of dust covered the floor for a foot or two beyond that wall, but the rest of the kitchen was clean and the white horizontal blinds looked very new. The bedrooms were a decent size, each with sufficient natural light but no view. Shayla caught

Paul's attention and arched her eyebrows. Paul subtly nodded his head in assent.

While Judi opened cupboards and Paul flicked on lights and tested faucets, Vicki summarized the refugee sponsorship.

"So is that like a group of five sponsorship?" Parvan asked. This was a means for any five or more adult Canadian or permanent residents to sponsor refugees. "My partner is Kurdish and we're thinking about helping some Kurdish refugees."

"Similar," Vicki replied. "Our church would be equivalent to the group of five, but we're dealing with an intermediary body, Canadian Lutheran World Relief, rather than directly with the government. It's one of the refugee agencies that have a special arrangement with the federal government. I don't understand how all this works. I just know that it saved us from having to handle a bunch of paperwork and gives us a backup organization. They're the people holding the money in trust for the family's living expenses for the first year."

As the conversation proceeded, it became clear that everyone was happy with the arrangement. Without an explicit decision to proceed, Parvan leaned on the kitchen counter and began filling in British Columbia's standard rental agreement form. "So whose names should I put on the form? We'll do another agreement when the family arrives."

"Put down my name for now," Paul said. "We're so grateful you're willing to do a one-month rental rather than a longer lease with an eventual sublease to the family. I brought the maximum cash I can withdraw in one day from my bank machine, $500, and I'll give you a cheque for the balance. The cash lets you know we're committed."

After clarifying which utilities and services were included in the basic rent, Paul and Shayla reviewed the form. "February 15 looks right for the start date, but what's with the September ending?" Shayla asked.

"Oops. I'll change that to March 15."

Paul signed the form. As there was no duplicate copy for him to take, he pulled his cell phone from his front pocket and carefully photographed the two pages of the form, checking the images before returning the form to Parvan. As they left, he murmured to Shayla that they had no written evidence that Parvan had committed to renting to the Mousas after his tenancy ended. "I'm feeling good about everything, but out of an abundance of caution, I'll send an email to Parvan as soon as I get home so that we have something in writing."

The essence of Paul's email to the landlord was that he would pay $1,500 for a one month rental. "I won't occupy the premises, so it's fine if the last of the renovations takes a little longer than planned." He would pick up the key at the end of February so the group could begin furnishing the suite. Then sometime during the Mousas' first week in Canada, they would meet with the landlord to sign the papers for the Mousas to rent in their own name.

Shayla replied immediately, "Nicely outlined, but I thought gas is included (I sent this only to you)."

"I thought so too at first," he replied, "but as she talked, the more it seemed she was confusing water (included) with the means for heating it. When she filled in the rental agreement, she didn't check the 'included in rent' box for natural gas. If we want to push back about this, my inclination is to wait until we're doing the Mousas' tenancy rather than jeopardize the goodwill we're establishing for the sake of saving a few dollars for one month."

What had caught his attention was Parvan's insistence on a six-month lease because he understood the trend was to annual leases. "This is a topic I'm not very well informed about, especially with respect to rent increases, so I'm a bit nervous even though it may be fine."

Shayla was not at all certain that the shorter term was a good thing. "I actually think a one-year lease is better for us, as it gives us the stability we need for the family. We can start applying for social housing only after a year. Would it be automatic renewal after six months or could she actually end the agreement then?"

"She said the concern driving the six-month period was only fear of bad tenants," Paul wrote. "That's understandable and I'm inclined to believe her. Hence my explicit mention that we're here to help resolve any problems. In any event, I included the word 'renewable' in the email I sent."

"Do you think we should look at the *Residential Tenancy Act* about the rights of both parties in case of a difference of opinion?"

"Yes. It's been over thirty years since I rented in BC and the world has changed. There's a fair number of protections, I believe. I'm not too worried about the Mousas having to move out after six or twelve months. My biggest anxieties at the moment are that they won't arrive as expected on March 7 and whether there will be any surprises such as serious depression or emotional trauma. However, we can cross those bridges when we get there. We're doing okay for the moment."

Shayla agreed that things were going well. "I hope we continue to enjoy this crazy ride. So far, we've yet to have a bad thing happen."

Travel Arrangements and Graft

Paul scratched his head as he studied Leandra's photo of her travel itinerary, a mere two lines in length. The cryptic airline and airport codes perplexed him. He printed the itinerary and tucked it in his shirt pocket to take to a travel agent to interpret. It seemed that the route might be from Beirut to Istanbul for a six-hour layover and then to Toronto for eighteen hours before leaving on a different airline for Vancouver. He failed to figure out even tentatively the duration of each of the three flights.

"The stopover in Toronto presents some interesting issues," Penny emailed. "Will Canada Border Services do all the processing in Toronto? Provide food and accommodation for the overnight stay there?" And then in Vancouver, she wondered whether the family would exit from an immigration office in the international terminal or appear in the domestic terminal with all the other passengers from Toronto. She closed by mentioning that when she flew Air Canada from Paris to Vancouver, she cleared customs during a layover in Montreal. "It was bewildering for us, and we're Canadian!"

The long period in Toronto also bothered Shayla. "I texted Leandra to warn her that they should prepare for an uncomfortable night in the airport, but they would finally be safe after all these years."

The next day's news proved more rattling, making concerns about sleeping on the floor of an airport lounge suddenly seem trivial and irrelevant. It appeared that local authorities might prohibit the Mousas from boarding their flight in Beirut, putting their entire journey to Canada at risk.

This startling information emerged almost casually when Shayla asked Natalie, the Syrian-Canadian contact in Surrey, if she knew how the long and complicated journey could be made more bearable for the family. "Natalie figures there will be several families travelling together, who can help each other. However, she told me that Leandra had confided in her that the family needs to pay money for the four years they've been living in Lebanon without a residency permit. Leandra was too shy to tell me herself. The amount is about $1,200." Shayla speculated that this financial demand was a way for government officials in a very overstretched country to squeeze some last money out of people as they left.

Karl replied first, wondering about the legitimacy of this significant surprise. "Given the language barrier, are we sure this is a real requirement from the Lebanese government and not just some kind of blackmail?" He was uncomfortable that neither Leandra nor CLWR had mentioned this before. "I know that Shayla and Leandra have an excellent rapport, so I suggest asking her directly. If she truly needs the money, we should definitely respond fully and quickly."

Gayle at Benediction said she would endorse using some of the money Benediction had donated for the exit fees. "I'm heading for a knee replacement tomorrow morning and will be out of the office until March 12, so I'm useless for this entire process."

Paul had heard of some Iranian refugees passing through Turkey who had faced a similar squeeze. "I assume this is like a bribe and perhaps unavoidable. It may be more a case of how best to respond so as not to get sucked into an additional surprise surtax." This, he remarked, was a firsthand experience for North Americans "of the yucky situations in so many parts of the world. I think Lebanon scores similarly to Guatemala and Nigeria on the world corruption index."

Shayla learned that Natalie had been texting in Arabic with Leandra. The $1,200 was in American funds but the Mousas had been able to obtain a portion of the money locally. Only her family knew that they have been receiving money from Canada.

"And Western Union and whoever that clerk chooses to tell," Vicki commented.

Canadian Lutheran World Relief offered to make some enquires, so the group agreed to sit tight and wait. The agency was aware that neighbourhood crime syndicates in certain African countries sometimes prevented refugees from going to their various screening interviews unless they paid for protection. It had not heard of such problems in Lebanon, though, and was unfamiliar with the extra costs there.

CLWR also forwarded a message it had received from the government on February 5 about permanent resident visas having been issued and the International Organization for Migration contacted for final resettlement arrangements. This included enrolling the Mousas in the Canadian Orientation Abroad course, assisting with any exit permit procedures, and booking travel. "It is estimated that these persons will arrive in Canada within four to ten weeks of the date of this notice. As per normal procedures, a

Notification of Arrival Transmission will be sent to you at least ten business days prior to arrival."

How is it that the Mousas already have their travel itinerary, Paul wondered, *but none of these international bodies is letting on to us that transportation has already been arranged? Too many links in the communication chain, I suppose.*

A couple of days later, Shayla reported that Leandra had $500 and needed another $700. Leandra had enquired at a government office and been told she had to pay exactly one week before their travel date or her family would not be allowed to leave the country. "I am quite sure," Shayla said, "they are living extremely frugally and are saving part of the stipends we've been sending."

Not exactly a typical Valentine message, Paul mused on February 14 as he wrote to say he hadn't heard from CLWR about the exit fee. "I'm torn about how proactive to be, partly because I realize bureaucracy is slow and partly because I don't want other organizations dumping their problems on us. My understanding is that the federal government is responsible for getting the family to their final destination and that our formal responsibility begins only at the Vancouver airport. However, I also want to be compassionate and sensitive to the family's situation before they reach us."

CLWR finally got back to Paul. "I spoke with a local Syrian about how and when to send the funds. He said it's appropriate and to send the $700 at any time, preferably sooner rather than later."

With the dilemma about the exit fee resolved, attention returned to the travel arrangements. "We can wire funds to Air Canada in Toronto so our family has some cash when they arrive in Canada," Penny said. "I'll call the airline and see what I can find out." She reached a helpful clerk and learned that the family would likely be processed in Toronto and assisted in getting to their next flight, and would probably arrive at the domestic terminal in Vancouver. "If we want, we can purchase prepaid meal vouchers from the airline."

Eventually, with the help of CLWR, the welcoming team determined that the Community Airport Newcomers Network would meet, feed, and house the Mousas in a hotel in Toronto, although the government would later bill the Mousas for the cost of this service. The All Saints hosts should indeed go to the domestic terminal of the Vancouver airport, with CLWR cautioning, "Don't be too early because they'll hold them to do the interim federal health paperwork and so on. It's just my suggestion based on experience."

Odds and Ends

Team meetings and conversations increasingly focused on logistical matters such as collecting donated furnishings, cutting extra keys for the suite, and coordinating with the Seattle partners who wanted to help clean and set up the home. Often the agendas covered familiar topics but with new twists as planning became more detailed and new information emerged.

Preparing to Relocate

– So what's with the photo of the certificate that Leandra sent?

– You mean the Canadian Orientation Abroad course they completed?

– I guess so. I don't remember the wording.

– That's a three-day course for refugees that the federal government funds to prepare refugees for life in Canada.

– Is that where they're told things like when you call the police, you don't have to pay money to get them to investigate? In fact, that's a very bad thing to do.

– Probably, I suppose so. See if you can Google it.

– Came right up, but it's the boring official version: "Encompasses essential topics such as employment, education, housing, health, life in Canada, access to citizenship, and settlement services."

– Hope the course wasn't as dull. Though, I suppose the clientele is super keen because this stuff really matters to them, so it probably doesn't matter how dynamic the instruction is. As long as the information is accurate and covers the important topics.

– It seems like a great service. There's so much for them to absorb and retain, and their first weeks in Canada will be overwhelming. It's good to get the orientation started well before they get here.

– You know, before I got involved in this project, I had no idea how much happens overseas. I thought refugees just sat in camps until their lucky number came up, and then they were shipped abroad. I had no idea about all the screening, the international organization that arranges travel, or the orientation course.

– I was every bit as clueless. But let me change the topic to a very practical matter that probably wasn't covered in the orientation course. How old is the little boy? Six or seven?

– Sounds about right. Why?

– Do you think he weighs seventy pounds? If not, we'll have to get a booster seat for the car.

– Oh, now there's something I hadn't thought about. If we do, I'll bet the Mousas will think we're nuts for refusing to drive without a booster.

– It might be hard for them even to accept that everybody has to buckle up and that we'll refuse to take more passengers than we have seat belts.

– I'm old enough to remember when seat belts became mandatory. There were a ton of Canadians who had trouble accepting that law. Changing topics again, do you think we should bring some food to the airport when we meet them?

– Why? If they or we are hungry, we can buy a sandwich easily enough.

– I know. It's more that food represents hospitality, regardless of whether anybody eats it.

Banking
– After the discussion at our last meeting, I did some more research about the bank and the credit union.
– So which would be better?
– I'm not clear. Each has strengths and weaknesses. The Royal Bank branch is closer and has a translation app.
– What do you mean?
– They're supposed to have an iPad that connects them with an interpreter elsewhere in Canada. So help in Arabic should always be available, in real time and letting you see body language.
– That's cool. Why wouldn't we open an account there?
– Maybe because the basic account costs $11 a month, unless you want to accept low service and pay $4 a month. So the trade-off is that the Royal is close and simple, but probably more expensive.
– And what do you think about the Vancity Credit Union?
– Figuring out the fee structure is tough if you don't keep a minimum monthly balance of $1,000, which our family probably won't.
– I have a Vancity account. If it's under $1,000, then the cost is $7 per month, and that gives you everything.
– Thanks, that helps. I got lost on the website trying to figure out what's included in what they call "everyday transactions." The credit union has a program for Syrian refugees, but I think it might be little more than the financial seminars they do with the Immigrant Services Society. And they offer an interest-free loan for the government travel and medical screening debt, but the government doesn't start charging interest on the loan for a couple of years. So I don't know how big an advantage that really is.
– What about translation? That's a big deal for me.
– Well, the Hampstead branch doesn't have an Arabic speaker, although they say they could phone headquarters and hope an Arabic speaker is available. The next branch over has somebody who knows Arabic, but they are a supervisor of some sort and don't do frontline banking.

– Bigger financial organizations have better services. That's just the way it is.

– While you've been talking, I looked on the Royal's website. They offer an account for newcomers to Canada that has no monthly fees for nine months.

– Well, let's start there, then. We could re-evaluate after six or so months.

– But switching institutions could be a pain, what with automatic deposits and so on.

– Switching might be the least of our problems. Let me pass on a story my daughter told me about the experience of some sponsors she knows on one of the Gulf Islands. Now granted, that's an isolated rural location that differs from ours, but the story is instructive.

– Sponsors of Syrians?

– Yes. It seems the family went shopping in Vancouver and drained their bank account. The sponsors were upset, but the family didn't trust banks. They feared they wouldn't get all their money back because of inflation or skimming, or whatever. Possessions, on the other hand, were a bird in hand.

– What did they buy? Did they drain their whole year's income?

– I don't know. I don't have those details. My point is simply that they saw the financial world in a way that would ever cross our minds. They didn't trust institutions the way we do. With the clan approach, if they run short, others in the family will help them out. They've lived this way their whole life.

– Doesn't mean our family will have that outlook, but it's worth keeping the possibility in mind.

Mental Health

– When you were at the airport five or six years ago to greet the Badawis, you said a number of them were crying. I find that so touching.

– Touching? It was disturbing. Those weren't tears of relief and happiness. They were hurting.

– Hurting?

– Well, yes. I think getting on that plane must have felt more like a funeral, the official end of life as they knew it, than a happy birth. We as sponsors were all excited and eager, but they were exhausted and their feelings were not the same as ours.

– No, you're right about not projecting our worldview on newcomers. I've been struck over these past months by how many local people seem to treat refugee sponsorship as Barbie dolls for grownups.

– Come again?

– Well, it's "Oh, boy, we get to outfit them. We can buy them clothes and fix up their house. And then we can take them around to meet and greet." It's like scripting a make-believe play for Barbie and Ken. They seem to lose sight that these are real, complex people who don't necessarily see things the way we do.

– Yes, it's a bit like the shopping thing, where people are only too happy to donate things but leery about meeting emotional needs such as simple friendship.

– Did you see the note Vicki sent around about supporting people with depression? Half the points were don'ts, things for us not to do: don't minimize their pain or make comparisons, don't offer advice or judge or offer tough love. It was really about being patient, being present, and just making small gestures. Simple friendship.

– And getting professional help.

– That too. After seeing what Vicki sent, I looked up survivor's guilt, because that might be something else we might have to deal with. I was flabbergasted to learn that, if survivor's guilt is left untreated, it can actually morph into full-blown PTSD.

– Seriously? My assumption was that any guilt would gradually diminish with time, so I suppose I would have just listened but not tried to encourage any sort of treatment.

- I think society's coming to recognize that ignoring any mental health issue is rarely a good idea.
- But that's often what happens in the church. We're good about supporting people with physical illnesses, but mental health is still in the closet. It's like depression is a personality defect or a sign of weak faith. It's one of our last taboos.
- True enough, but in fairness, sometimes the issue isn't mental health. Sometimes the person is just too self-absorbed and lacking perspective. In those cases, a prod or walking alongside them might be all that's needed.
- Which brings me back to the point about seeing people as real, complex human beings, not as stereotypes. Until you know a person well, you can't tell whether they're facing a genuine mental illness or just experiencing the normal ups and downs of life.
- Regardless, talking openly about these issues takes away their power and the shame.

Schedule
- Okay, so where are we with the first week's schedule and only doing one or two things per day?
- They arrive at Amelia's house in the evening of March 7. The next day is just rest and exploring the local area by way of orientation. What did we settle on for Friday the ninth?
- Meet with the school settlement person to get the registration process started, assuming I can get an appointment.
- One more thing about schools: the kids might not be allowed in without proof that they have all the right immunizations.
- But didn't they get medical checks already in Lebanon?
- Yes, but knowing they don't currently have communicable or tropical diseases isn't the same as ensuring they have the mumps or measles vaccinations, or whatever else is required here in Vancouver.
- So what is required?

- I don't know. That's part of why I think it's good to meet with the school settlement person as soon as possible. They'll tell us what's needed or who to go to in order to find out.
- Then where do they go to get shots? We don't have a doctor yet.
- The ISS Welcome Centre in Vancouver has an immunization clinic for newcomers. That might be our best bet.
- So how about tentatively seeing if we can go there on Wednesday the fourteenth?
- Sounds good. They may also be able to tell us about applying for the provincial health care card, because the federal plan is only temporary for a few months.
- But the federal plan is supposed to have better coverage, so they should use it for as long as possible before switching to the provincial one.
- I'm pretty sure that, to apply provincially, you need a BC services card. It will have to be separate from the driver's licence because they won't be driving yet.
- But you go to the same place to get both cards.
- Yes, and it's drop-in. No appointments. The wait can be really long, so perhaps go mid-week in the morning when it's less likely to be busy.
- There's something you forgot on the eighth. We arranged to meet the landlord then to sign the tenancy papers. The Mousas need that agreement before the schools will start processing the kids. The appointment is at 7:00. Penny and I won't be able to attend at that time. That's why I had initially suggested 8:00.
- No problem. I'm available then.
- Alright now, what about the weekend?
- Saturday, they can spend more time in the suite. Perhaps we could get the phones sorted out then.
- Do you think I could bring them to church on Sunday? Not to introduce them, because that could be too overwhelming. Just nip in and out.

– I suppose so, but remember that our style of worship may be very foreign to them. As I understand Orthodox worship, there's no point where everybody is sitting quietly, waiting for a starting hymn. Things can go on for hours, with people coming and going. Constant singing, venerating Mary, kissing icons. Just because they're Christian doesn't mean they're similar to us.

– Isn't that the Sunday when Natalie has invited us, the grand all of us, to her house for supper?

– Yes, that's so nice. I'll keep track of who wants to go so I can give her numbers.

– Back to the schedule. We really have to try to get an appointment on Monday the thirteenth with the little Hampstead office of Immigrant Services Society. That's the only day of the week when they have an Arabic speaker who will help us complete forms and make sure we have a current checklist of everything that needs to be done.

– So what's left on our must-do-right-away list? I'm thinking just the language assessment for the parents and opening whatever bank account we decide on.

– Can we maybe not schedule those? Just play them by ear, knowing they have to be dealt with early on?

– Why are you saying that? Is something bothering you?

– It's just that life doesn't follow all our tidy little plans. What if they pick up a bug on the plane and get sick when they arrive? That's pretty common. Or they're overwhelmed and start shutting down. I'm not suggesting anything will necessarily go off track. Just that, it's a possibility and we need to be able to adjust to it.

– Fair enough. And I suppose that after waiting years to get here, if something happens a day or two later than we'd envisaged, it really doesn't matter.

– We're so Western and task-oriented. Our culture is showing. In Syrian culture, punctuality is probably valued much less than here.

Communications Technology
– Pay-as-you-go might be the cheapest way to get them started with a cell phone plan. Phones for the two parents and at least the oldest child. I'm assuming they'll arrive with usable phones and we'll just need to get SIM cards and a plan.
– Too bad we couldn't get an American plan. Canada's cell phone coverage is way more expensive than in most countries.
– My son-in-law suggested a bundle is the best way to go for cablevision and internet service. I'm presuming no landline phone.
– Why get cablevision? We don't have a TV, and they can get all they need by streaming on the internet. TV isn't the only way to watch movies anymore to improve one's English. Cablevision is too much of a luxury for people who will be living on the edge of poverty. I'd rather show them the library computers and just equip them with a cell phone, and take it from there.
– I can't imagine that would be convenient, assuming they could get there when the library is open. Maybe smart phones are sufficient but using desktop computers at the library is an obsolete strategy from decades ago.
– In talking with the landlord, she said she'd see if she could arrange to share internet costs with the upstairs tenants, assuming there's decent reception down below.
– Say, have you played around very much with Google Translate? It's amazing.
– I know. Not only have I downloaded the entire Arabic–English dictionary to my phone so that it's available even when I'm offline, but it will speak sentences and even seems to have some ability to accept spoken input. One dialect option is Lebanese Arabic.
– And maybe it will accept input from a stylus or fingernail on devices with a touchscreen. Good for somebody who doesn't know the English keyboard and has to hunt and peck.

– This may not be snazzy and interactive like Translate, but it's also great that the Arabic version of the BC government guide for new immigrants is posted online.

Countdown

March 4, 2018

Shayla's attention drifted from the prayer of thanksgiving as she contemplated how best to summarize the previous day's work party. As of 5:00 p.m. on Saturday, everything was ready in the Mousas' new home. Except, she corrected herself, for the kitchen table and chairs that Vicki's son would deliver in a day or two. The donations had been generous, resulting in the happy problem of determining how best to distribute the surplus. A dozen volunteers had shown up, many staying for the entire day.

For some reason, the choir members, who had earlier moved to sit with their families following the anthem, were now reassembling next to the piano. The closing hymn was familiar, and a livelier one than the dirges that frequently characterized the Lenten services, so why were they there? The congregation didn't need musical leadership for this song.

The pianist continued after the last verse and the choir began the encore, some extra lines about springing clocks forward next weekend for daylight savings time. I guess the announcements have begun, Shayla concluded with a slight grin. She strolled to the lectern on the other side of the sanctuary and waited while two others spoke.

When Shayla's turn came, she launched right in. "My, what a wonderful day Saturday was! We had four American friends join in the fun of moving furniture, picking up donations, schlepping all sorts of furnishings, and setting up each room in the Mousa family's new home. The family is arriving, if flights go as scheduled, this

Wednesday afternoon. They'll move into the suite in the next week or two, and we're ready for them."

She scanned the congregation. "I can't say enough thank yous to everybody for your ideas, your prayers, your monetary donations, your very practical gifts, for helping to clean and move, and generally being there for this family over the last little while. It's very humbling and I'm so grateful. The whole welcoming team is so very grateful to you.

"The real work with the family is about to begin. Over the coming weeks and months, they'll need a great deal of support from us. Not support that will make them dependent on us, but assistance in becoming competent and independent. We'll keep you posted about opportunities for helping with this phase of the sponsorship.

"The green poster board at the back has some suggestions on how to become involved, meeting the family in their own home or having them over for tea and a walk, for example. The suggestions are all normal things that will help them feel welcome and cared for. This, I think, is at the heart of what the Gospel calls us to do, and All Saints is heeding that call."

Monday's news was rather less upbeat. Shayla dialled Amelia's number. "I just spoke with Natalie. She tells me that Leandra is extremely nervous about staying with you when they first arrive for fear of imposing on you and your husband. She's worried her kids will make too much noise and agitate the neighbours."

"Well, that might be how she expresses her anxiety, but I don't think we're likely to upset the neighbours. I wonder what the real issues are?"

"I'm not sure. I asked Natalie to reassure them about your hospitality and about the size of your house. With your kids gone, there are plenty of extra beds."

"And about the many appointments in the first week they need to be taken to?"

"Of course."

"Sounds like my most important job may simply be to help them feel welcome and relaxed. I hope I'm up to it."

An hour after talking with Amelia, Shayla was still perturbed. She spoke again to Natalie and then sent a note to the welcoming team, asking whether it might be best to let the Mousas decide when they arrived where they wanted to spend their first few nights. She added that Natalie was keen to accompany the family from the airport to Amelia's house to assist with translation. "As a little aside, I asked the school secretary if they had spare booster seats. They did and sent one home inscribed 'To the Mousa family from Clearwater Elementary.'"

Vicki viewed Leandra's anxiety as a healthy sign that she was being realistic about the challenges of moving into a new language and culture. "I've found it hard enough as a paying tourist in a foreign country to spend a single night in a homestay, trying to understand routines, not give offence, and engage socially. I think it would be very good for Natalie to come to Amelia's house on Wednesday as we feed and organize them."

Paul, the official tenant for the first half of March of the suite rented for the Mousas, said they could move into the suite as his guests after a short stay at Amelia's. "But not for the first couple of nights. They need to be rested and sufficiently oriented so that they're not likely to cause the stupid accidents of leaving taps running or stove elements on that overwhelmed people can make." He also thought they needed a cell phone so they would not be cut off from help. "We can't rely entirely on the upstairs tenants in emergencies."

Tuesday arrived, the day when the Mousas were scheduled to board a Turkish Airways flight from Beirut to Istanbul and then on to Canada. "Has anyone, such as CLWR, heard what's happening with our family?" Penny asked. "Why haven't we had a text from anybody? Does anybody know if they arrived in Toronto this afternoon?"

Judi replied immediately. "I just left a message at the CLWR office. I haven't heard back." She attempted to put a positive spin on the situation. "Sometimes no news is good news. Let's hope that's the case for us."

Wishful thinking was not the type of reassurance Penny sought. Shoulders hunched and jaw tight, she searched the web for a Canadian telephone number. "I just talked with Turkish Airlines," she wrote thirty minutes later. "The customer service rep confirmed that the five members of the Mousa family checked in for both flights yesterday. As far as he could tell, they arrived in Toronto at 3:30 Eastern time this afternoon! He said there was nothing showing as unusual."

The family still faced a mountain of challenges, but they were safe. Safe after expulsion from their home in Syria four years ago. Safe after living in the shadow of a Lebanese society that treated them as non-persons. Protected now in Canada from violence and outright exploitation, soon to meet individuals in Vancouver who were both able and willing to provide assistance. Many silent prayers of thanks were offered in Ontario, British Columbia, and Washington State.

Wednesday morning came and went with no further news. Karl, William, and Amy started their journey from Seattle regardless, a little before the flight from Toronto had even departed. Paul also left early for Vancouver in order to stop on his way to the airport and see the condominium unit his daughter had bought the previous day. Pastor Ellen planned to swing by the airport between meetings to say hello to everybody, even if she couldn't stay long. Penny remained at work to submit a tender before the deadline. Life, as it always does, went on despite the little dramas that occur in international airports.

Air Canada Flight 115 reached the gate at YVR fifteen minutes ahead of schedule. Two volunteers in green vests at an information table in the domestic arrivals area thought the Mousas would likely enter through the doors to the left. The fifteen people who had shown up to greet the newcomers therefore drifted in small groups to the farthest baggage carousel.

"Are you sure this is right? The carousel for the Toronto flight is over there."

"No, I'm not sure. This is just what the volunteers thought. The Mousas are supposed to be escorted out, and we have to sign for them. There's no guarantee they'll appear where their luggage does."

Half an hour passed, during which crowds of passengers waited by the carousels and retrieved their luggage. "I think all the Toronto passengers have deplaned and cleared out. Where's our family? Do you think something's wrong?"

"It's probably just officialdom. I expect there's paperwork here and not only in Toronto."

A half wall with swinging gates separated the public area from the passenger arrival space. The carousels were largely empty and only a few people milled in the arrival area. The members of the welcoming delegation who felt they could claim they were semi-official—Oreva from CLWR, Natalie and Rona as interpreters, and Shayla as the All Saints signatory—slipped through the gates and strolled towards a set of frosted glass doors. Nobody challenged them and soon four others sidled in to join them.

"Go on in," Ellen said to Karl and William. "You have a strong moral claim to be the first to greet the Mousas. I'll stay here and watch the balloons and your bags."

Ten minutes later, the doors opened. "You're here!" exclaimed Natalie in Arabic, her arms outstretched. "Welcome. Welcome to your new home and friends in Canada."

EPILOGUE

The Mousas' arrival in Vancouver was subdued but warm. A few tears, many hugs, and too many photos. It took a while to find a cart, gather luggage, decide who was going to travel in which vehicle, and actually leave the airport. But leave we did and a new chapter began.

One week before the Mousas' arrival, revised federal government policy greatly relaxed the repayment schedule and interest-free period for the $8,500 travel and medical loan to the Mousas.

I want to tell you what happened next, but that story is not mine to tell. Perhaps one day, a member of the Mousa family will choose to share these details. Perhaps not. Regardless, if you talk with neighbours who immigrated to a new land or read memoirs of refugee experiences, you can make a few educated guesses as to what the subsequent months held for the Mousa family.

I also want to tell you exactly how two years of deciding and preparing to sponsor a Syrian refugee family changed and enriched a group of Canadians and Americans, but I don't yet have anywhere near the full story. I've given you a slightly fictionalized account of the little that I observed, but this is just the start of the storytelling. Let's keep the conversation going.

Let's hear from one another how pain and suffering, whether in a war-torn country halfway around the world or close to home, can be transformed into the birth of something good and beautiful. Such stories are at the heart of the Christian faith.